Doing Archaeology
in the Land of the Bible

Doing Archaeology in the Land of the Bible

A BASIC GUIDE

John D. Currid

Baker Books

A Division of Baker Book House Co
Grand Rapids, Michigan 49516

© 1999 by John D. Currid

Published by Baker Books
a division of Baker Book House Company
P.O. Box 6287, Grand Rapids, MI 49516-6287

Printed in the United States of America

Library of Congress Cataloging-in-Publication Data

Currid, John D., 1951–
    Doing archaeology in the land of the Bible : a basic guide / John D.
Currid.
        p.   cm.
    Includes bibliographical references and index.
    ISBN 0-8010-2213-4 (paper)
    1. Israel—Antiquities Popular works. 2. Excavations (Archaeology)—Israel Popular works. 3. Archaeology—Israel Popular works.
I. Title.
DS111.C95   1999
933—dc21   99-30489

For information about academic books, resources for Christian leaders, and all new releases available from Baker Book House, visit our web site:
http://www.bakerbooks.com

To My Father
Raymond E. Currid (1920–87)

Contents

Illustrations

Map

Figures

Preface

As a faculty member at Reformed Theological Seminary and an adjunct instructor at the Jerusalem Center for Biblical Studies, I have taught archaeology to hundreds of students within the land of Israel. Among them have been collegians, seminarians, alumni, and friends of the schools. In addition, I have served on the staff of major digs in the Middle East: Carthage, Tell el-Hesi, Bethsaida, and Lahav (as director of the agricultural project). During those excavations a primary responsibility of my work was to instruct students in the art and craft of archaeology. A glaring need became apparent in all those years of fieldwork: a handbook to introduce the student to the basics of the archaeology of the land of the Bible. In other words, I felt a great need for a book that would explain the fundamentals of archaeology to people who know little or nothing about the subject. That heartfelt need was the genesis of this present work.

Given that purpose, it goes without saying that this look at archaeology is not meant to be exhaustive. It is for the novice, with the hope of instilling interest, understanding, even passion for the topic. I truly hope that this little book will encourage readers to travel to Israel with the intention of taking up the spade. May it serve as a catalyst stimulating people to help uncover the remains of the past!

It is always difficult to acknowledge properly those who helped in the preparation of a manuscript. At the outset I would like to express my gratitude and everlasting affection to my two great friends and partners in Israel, Andy Hoffecker (RTS–Jackson) and

Reggie Kidd (RTS–Orlando). Next year in Jerusalem! May we never again order a pepperoni pizza in the holy city!

Reformed Theological Seminary has always encouraged my work in Israel and my writing projects. I want to thank our seminary president, Luder Whitlock, and his wife Mary Lou, both of whom traveled with me to Israel. Allen Curry, our academic dean, who also went with us to Israel, has been a continual source of inspiration and leadership. In addition, I wish to thank the board of Reformed Theological Seminary for granting me a sabbatical leave in order to complete this work.

I am grateful to my student assistants of the past few years for their tireless efforts in tutoring Hebrew and making corrections on this book: Albert Bisson, Steve Britt, and Inawaty Teddy. May God bless your future ministries!

It is a pleasure to acknowledge both Jim Weaver and Ray Wiersma of Baker Book House. Without their unfailing labor this book would never have gone to press. Thank you.

Most of all I want to thank my wife Nancy. While this book was being produced, she took the brunt of the work at home by running the house and homeschooling the children. Time and again she went above and beyond the call of duty.

Finally, this book would never have seen the light of day without all those who traveled with me over the years to the Middle East. All your comments, suggestions, and questions were important in the formation of this manuscript. May your knowledge of and walk with Christ have been enhanced because of your trip to Israel.

Abbreviations

AA	*American Antiquity*
ABD	*Anchor Bible Dictionary*, ed. D. N. Freedman (6 vols., 1992)
ASOR Newsletter	*American Schools of Oriental Research Newsletter*
AUSS	*Andrews University Seminary Studies*
BA	*Biblical Archaeologist*
BAR	*Biblical Archaeology Review*
BASOR	*Bulletin of the American Schools of Oriental Research*
BJPES	*Bulletin of the Jewish Palestine Exploration Society*
BR	*Bible Review*
EI	*Eretz-Israel*
HTR	*Harvard Theological Review*
IDB	*Interpreter's Dictionary of the Bible*
IEJ	*Israel Exploration Journal*
JBL	*Journal of Biblical Literature*
JNES	*Journal of Near Eastern Studies*
JPOS	*Journal of the Palestine Oriental Society*
PEFQS	*Palestine Exploration Fund Quarterly Statement*
PEQ	*Palestine Exploration Quarterly*
TA	*Tel Aviv*
TB	*Tyndale Bulletin*
WA	*World Archaeology*
ZDPV	*Zeitschrift des deutschen Palästina-Vereins*

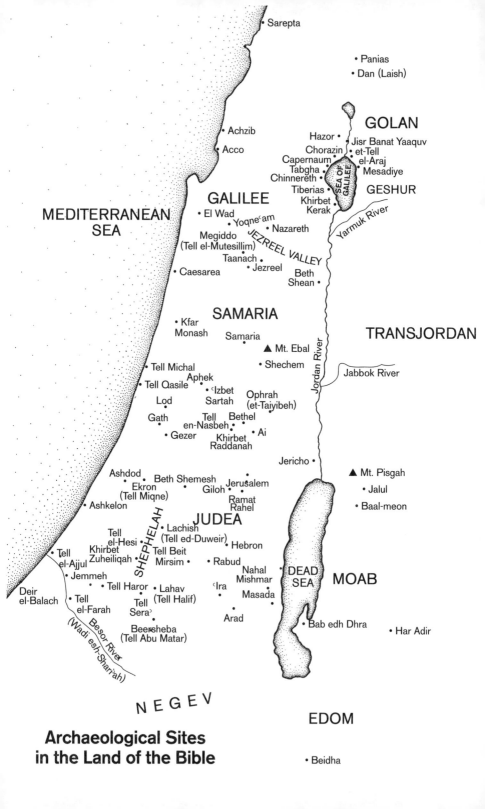

• Sarepta

• Panias
• Dan (Laish)

GOLAN

Achzib •

Hazor •
Chorazin •   Jisr Banat Yaaquv
Capernaum •   • et-Tell
Acco •   Tabgha •   el-Araj
Chinnereth •   Mesadiye
Tiberias •   SEA OF GALILEE
Khirbet   GESHUR
Kerak •

GALILEE

• El Wad
Yoqne'am •
• Nazareth
Megiddo
(Tell el-Mutesillim)   JEZREEL VALLEY   Yarmuk River
Taanach •
• Jezreel
• Caesarea   Beth
Shean •

MEDITERRANEAN
SEA

SAMARIA

• Kfar
Monash   Samaria
•   TRANSJORDAN
▲ Mt. Ebal
• Shechem

Tell Michal •   Jordan River
Aphek   Jabbok River
• Tell Qasile   • 'Izbet
Lod   Sartah   Ophrah
(et-Taiyibeh)
Gath   Tell   Bethel
• en-Nasbeh •
• Gezer   • Ai
Khirbet
Raddanah

Jericho •

Ashdod •   ▲ Mt. Pisgah
Beth Shemesh •   Jerusalem •
Ekron   Giloh •   • Jalul
(Tell Miqne)   Ramat
• Baal-meon
• Ashkelon   Rahel
JUDEA
Lachish
Tell   • Lachish
el-Hesi •   (Tell ed-Duweir) •   Hebron
Khirbet   Tell Beit
• Tell   Zuheiliqah   Mirsim •   • Rabud
el-Ajjul   Nahal   DEAD
• Jemmeh   Mishmar   SEA   MOAB
Deir   • Tell Haror   • Lahav   'Ira •
el-Balach   • Tell   (Tell Halif)   Masada •
el-Farah   Tell
Sera'   Arad •   • Bab edh Dhra   • Har Adir
Beersheba •
(Tell Abu Matar)

Besor River
(Wadi esh-Shari'ah)

N E G E V

EDOM

**Archaeological Sites
in the Land of the Bible**

• Beidha

What in the World Is Archaeology?

1

What exactly is archaeology? The term conjures up a variety of images. To some it implies romantic adventure: the search for long-lost civilizations, for the definitive interpretation of the Shroud of Turin, and for the location of Noah's ark. Others see archaeology as a thing of the past. It evokes images of a khaki-clad Westerner donning a pith helmet and examining dry and dusty remains. To still others it suggests grinning skeletons, missing links, and poisonous snakes (who can forget Indiana Jones's comment, "Not snakes! I hate snakes!"?). Popular visions of archaeology sometimes border on the bizarre. For example, inasmuch as "no man knows [Moses'] burial place to this day" (Deut. 34:6), I was once asked to equip an expedition to find his bones in the land of Moab. Pyramid power, extraterrestrial spaceships, and King Tut's curse are viewed as part of the archaeologist's domain. Children may say that they want to grow up to be archaeologists because of the glamour and adventure involved.

None of those ideas is close to the truth, and they do no justice to the practice of archaeology today. One hundred fifty years ago the notion of archaeology as adventure and glamour may have been more accurate; even serious work back then was no more than mere treasure-hunting. The modus operandi at that time was "to recover as many valuables as possible in the shortest time" (Fagan 1978, 3). But what about today? What is archaeology all about?

The term *archaeology* derives from two Greek words: *archaios*, which means "ancient, from the beginning," and *logos*, "a word." Etymologically, therefore, it signifies a word about or study of antiquity. And that is how the term was employed by ancient writers. Plato, for example, notes that the Lacedaemonians "are very fond of hearing about the genealogies of heroes and men, Socrates, and the foundations of cities in ancient times and, in short, about archaeology in general" (*Hippias* 285d). In the introduction to the *History of the Peloponnesian War* Thucydides summarizes the earlier history of Greece under the title "Archaeology." Denis of Halicarnassus wrote a history of Rome called *Roman Archaeology*. Similarly, Josephus called his history of the Jews *Archaeology*. The fact is, the word "archaeology" was "synonymous with ancient history" (de Vaux 1970, 65).

Archaeology: *the study of objects used by past societies.*

The modern sense of the word "archaeology" is much different. Archaeology is the study of the material remains of the past (Chippindale 1996, 42). It is concerned with the physical, the material side of life. "Archaeology, therefore, is limited to the *realia*, but it studies all the *realia*, from the greatest classical monuments to the locations of prehistoric fireplaces, from art works to small everyday utensils . . . in short, everything which exhibits a trace of the presence or activity of man. Archaeology seeks, describes, and classifies these materials" (de Vaux 1970, 65). This physical focus is underscored by Stuart Piggott's dictum that "archaeology is the science of rubbish."

The aim of archaeology is to discover, rescue, observe, and preserve buried fragments of antiquity and to use them to help reconstruct ancient life. It aids our perception of humankind's "complex and changing relationship with [the] environment" (Fagan 1978, 18). Archaeology can speak to every aspect of ancient society, whether it be government, cult, animal husbandry, agriculture, or whatever. It is, in short, "the method of finding out about the past of the human race in its material aspects, and the study of the products of this past" (Kenyon 1957, 9).

The discipline of archaeology has a very practical application for us. It tells us where we have come from and how we have developed; it provides very detailed information about our history. Archaeology can also serve as a barometer of the future. As George Santayana observed, whoever does not know history is bound to repeat it.

The written materials of antiquity do not belong to the field of archaeology proper. Written records are more the province of historians than archaeologists. Although the latter often dig up the written works, analysis and study thereof belong to the epigraphers, paleographers, and historians. The "importance of archaeology obviously decreases as written records become more plentiful" (Avi-Yonah 1974, 1).

Archaeology, then, is an auxiliary science of history. It is the handmaid of history, helping its study by revealing necessary information (Wiseman and Yamauchi 1979, 4). In fact, it provides data that written records normally do not. Ancient writing was restricted to an elite class and frequently biased (Chippindale 1996, 43). Archaeology by contrast describes and explains to us how all types of people lived, from the agricultural peasant to the king on his throne. Archaeology is no respecter or discriminator of class. Rather, it broadens our understanding of antiquity in ways that written documents cannot.

Archaeology is often considered to be a social science. It is in fact "the sole discipline in the social sciences concerned with reconstructing and understanding human behavior on the basis of the material remains left by our prehistoric and historic forebears" (Michaels 1996, 42). Accordingly, it is categorized in the United States as one of the four subdisciplines of anthropology, along with cultural anthropology, physical anthropology, and linguistics. Because of its focus, however, archaeology remains singular among the social sciences.

As a social science, archaeology is, of course, not an exact or natural science along the lines of chemistry or physics (Wiseman and Yamauchi 1979, 4). Not as systematic as those fields, it is necessarily more subjective and selective in its analysis and interpretation.

The study of archaeology has four basic divisions:

1. *Prehistoric archaeology* is concerned with the material remains of human activity before written records.
2. *Preclassical archaeology* focuses on the eastern Mediterranean and the Levant. It studies the ancient societies that developed in Egypt, Mesopotamia, and Palestine.
3. *Classical archaeology* concentrates on Greco-Roman civilizations.
4. *Historical archaeology* attempts to supplement written texts by describing the day-to-day operation of the cultures that produced them. A large subsection is called industrial archae-

ology because it focuses upon Western societies since the Industrial Revolution.

Archaeological method itself is subdivided into two parts: exploration and excavation. It is not always necessary to excavate in order to obtain valuable information about antiquity. Much can be gleaned from surface examination. But excavation is, of course, preferable because it provides deeper (!) and broader information.

The Beginnings of Archaeology

Modern archaeological excavation started with organized digs at Herculaneum (1738), located along the Bay of Naples (Albright 1957, 26). Tunnels dug at Herculaneum led to the recovery of magnificent statuary now housed in the Naples Museum. Karl Weber drew some very accurate architectural plans during these early excavations. The digs were eventually suspended at Herculaneum because of the great problem of having to chop through meters of volcanic residue that covered the site.

Excavations at Pompeii soon followed (1748). The first buildings to be excavated included "the smaller theatre (or Odeon, 1764), the Temple of Isis (1764), the so-called Gladiators' barracks (1767), and the Villa of Diomedes outside the Herculaneum Gate (1771)" (Gersbach 1996, 275).

Hieroglyphics: *Egyptian pictographic writing.*

Systematic archaeological work in the Near East did not begin until the turn to the nineteenth century. In 1798 Napoleon invaded Egypt. He brought with him a scientific expedition of scholars and draftsmen whose purpose was to survey the ancient monuments of Egypt. The account of their discoveries was published in 1809–13 as *Description de l'Egypte*. This first exploration was important because it opened the eyes of Europe to a vast ancient civilization. What Napoleon said to his troops as they stood beneath the pyramids was really intended for all Europe: "Fifty centuries look down upon you!"

The most significant find of the Napoleonic excursion was the Rosetta Stone (1799). It proved to be invaluable because it was the key to unlocking ancient Egyptian hieroglyphics, a picture script unutilized for over fourteen hundred years. Dating to the time of King Ptolemy V (204–180 B.C.), the Rosetta Stone is inscribed in three scripts: demotic,

> Rosetta Stone: *inscribed stone that provided the key for the decipherment of Egyptian hieroglyphics.*

Greek, and hieroglyphs. The Greek proved to be a translation of the ancient Egyptian language on the stone. The linguistic study of the Rosetta Stone by the English physician Thomas Young (1819) and the Frenchman Jean-François Champollion (1822) "marked the beginning of the scientific reading of hieroglyphs and the first step

Figure 1
The Ages of Antiquity

Ancient Palestine	Ancient Egypt	Ancient Mesopotamia
Neolithic 7000–4000		
Chalcolithic 4000–3200		
Early Bronze Age	Early Dynastic Period	
EB I 3200–2800	2920–2575	Early Dynastic Period
EB II 2800–2600		2700–2400
EB III 2600–2350	Old Kingdom	Akkad, Ur III
	2575–2134	2400–2000
EB IV 2350–2200		
Middle Bronze Age		
MB I 2200–2000	First Intermediate Period	
	2134–2040	
MB II 2000–1550	Middle Kingdom	Old Babylonian/Old
	2040–1640	Assyrian 2000–1600
Late Bronze Age	Second Intermediate	
	Period 1640–1532	
LB I 1550–1400	New Kingdom	Middle Babylonian/Middle
	1550–1070	Assyrian 1600–1000
LB II 1400–1200		
Iron Age		
Iron I 1200–1000	Third Intermediate Period	Neo-Babylonian/Neo-
	1070–712	Assyrian 1155–539
Iron II 1000–586	Late Period 712–343	
Persian 539–332		Persian 539–332
Hellenistic 323–37		Seleucid Era 312–141
Roman 37–A.D. 324		Parthian 141–A.D. 228

toward formulation of a system of ancient Egyptian grammar, the basis of modern Egyptology" (Andrews 1996, 620). Thus the first true archaeological find in the Near East was one of the greatest and most critical discoveries in the history of the discipline!

Archaeology and the Bible

The archaeology of the Bible is generally understood to fall under the category of preclassical archaeology, and to be a subdivision of Syro-Palestinian archaeology. Whereas the latter covers prehistoric times through the medieval period in Syria-Palestine, biblical archaeology focuses primarily on the Bronze Age, the Iron Age, and the Persian, Hellenistic, and Roman periods in that land. Most events recorded in the Bible occurred within that temporal setting.

The Early Bronze Age (c. 3200–2200 B.C.) was characterized by urbanization, a shift from village life to city dwelling. More settlements appeared in this age than at any time previously, and they were fortified. Full-fledged agricultural production, both fruits and vegetables, also became a major part of life in Palestine. A brisk international trade network was in evidence, especially with Egypt. This was the time of the first great empire building in the ancient Near East with grand states formed in Mesopotamia and Egypt.

The Middle Bronze Age (c. 2200–1550 B.C.) began with a period of decline. Palestine was populated mainly by pastoralists and villagers. Around 2000 B.C., however, a revival occurred, resulting in "the establishment of the Canaanite culture, which flourished during most of the second millennium B.C.E. [Before the Christian Era] and then gradually disintegrated during the last three centuries of that millennium. The second half of MB II [Middle Bronze II] was one of the most prosperous periods in the history of this culture, perhaps even its zenith" (Mazar 1990, 174). Indeed, this period was distinguished by a revolution in almost every aspect of material remains, including architecture, pottery, and patterns of settlement. Many scholars date the patriarchs of the Bible and the beginning of the Hebrew sojourn in Egypt to the latter phase of the Middle Bronze Age.

The Late Bronze Age (c. 1550–1200 B.C.) continued much of the material tradition, though the high culture of the Middle Bronze Age was beginning to erode and evaporate. There was a general decline in urbanization. Most of the settlements, for example, did not even have walls (Gonen 1984, 70). Many researchers fix the Hebrew exodus and conquest of the land of Canaan at the middle or end of the Late Bronze Age. Predominant in the archaeological investigations of Palestine during the Iron Age (c. 1200–586 B.C.) are remains from the Hebrew presence in the land. Included are materials from the periods of the judges, the united monarchy, and the two kingdoms of Israel and Judah. The Iron Age ended with the destruction of the southern kingdom and its capital Jerusalem in 586 B.C.

The next three periods (Persian, Hellenistic, and Roman) concern Palestine when under the domination of foreign powers. Accordingly, the archaeological remains from those periods reflect great foreign influence. Included in this era are the intertestamental and New Testament periods, with which the Bible and hence biblical archaeology reach their terminus ad quem.

Bibliography

Albright, W. F. 1957. *From the Stone Age to Christianity*. 2d ed. Garden City, N.Y.: Doubleday.

Andrews, C. A. R. 1996. "Rosetta Stone." In *The Oxford Companion to Archaeology*, ed. B. Fagan, 619–20. New York: Oxford University Press.

Avi-Yonah, M., ed. 1974. *Archaeology*. Jerusalem: Keter.

Chippindale, C. 1996. "Archaeology in the Contemporary World." In *The Oxford Companion to Archaeology*, ed. B. Fagan, 42–44. New York: Oxford University Press.

Fagan, B. 1978. *Quest for the Past*. Prospect Heights, Ill.: Waveland.

Gersbach, E. 1996. "Herculaneum and Pompeii." In *The Oxford Companion to Archaeology*, ed. B. Fagan, 274–75. New York: Oxford University Press.

Gonen, R. 1984. "Urban Canaan in the Late Bronze Period." *BASOR* 253:61–73.

Kenyon, K. 1957. *Beginning in Archaeology*. New York: Praeger.

Mazar, A. 1990. *Archaeology of the Land of the Bible*. New York: Doubleday.

Michaels, G. 1996. "Archaeology as a Discipline." In *The Oxford Companion to Archaeology*, ed. B. Fagan, 42. New York: Oxford University Press.

Vaux, R. de. 1970. "On Right and Wrong Uses of Archaeology." In *Near Eastern Archaeology in the Twentieth Century*, ed. J. A. Sanders, 64–80. Garden City, N.Y.: Doubleday.

Wiseman, D. J., and E. Yamauchi. 1979. *Archaeology and the Bible*. Grand Rapids: Zondervan.

A Brief History of Palestinian Archaeology

2

Archaeology as practiced in Palestine today is much different from what it was at its inception in the mid-nineteenth century. Originally, archaeology consisted of one or two Westerners who, with compass in hand, rode on horses throughout Palestine in an effort to identify and mark ancient sites from the Bible. Presently, however, the discipline is ruled by modern technology, with computer analysis and data organization at the forefront. Given the great expansion of archaeological fieldwork, information is exploding. Archaeology has been further revolutionized by incorporating many of the natural and social sciences into its investigations. How did such a revolution occur in a mere one hundred fifty years? How did the discipline evolve into what it is today? This chapter will provide a cursory outline of the history of archaeological research in Palestine.

Phase 1: Individual Investigation (1838—65)

The archaeological study of Palestine began with topographic surveys and historical-geographical studies during the nineteenth century (Mazar 1990, 10). The American scholar Edward Robinson (1794–1863) was the first to conduct systematic surface surveys of the land. Because of his great success in identifying ancient sites and in describing the geography of Palestine, he is generally regarded as "the founder of the scientific topography of Palestine" (King 1983, 55).

> Topography: *the study of the surface features of a region.*

As a student at Andover Theological Seminary in Massachusetts, Robinson came under the influence of one of the great Hebraists of the early nineteenth century, Moses Stuart. Robinson proved to be an able scholar, and at the urging of Stuart, he left to study in Europe for four years (1826–30). In Germany, Robinson sat under the great scholars Wilhelm Gesenius and Emil Roediger, and he learned geography with the incomparable Karl Ritter (Albright 1949, 25). On his return to America, Robinson began to formulate a plan: "I had long meditated the preparation of a work on biblical geography, and wished to satisfy myself by personal observation as to points on which I could find no information in the books of travellers" (Robinson 1856, 1:36). His plan was to travel throughout Palestine and to provide a systematic description of its geography and topography (Alt 1939, 375).

In 1838 Robinson traveled to the Middle East with his companion Eli Smith, an American missionary to Beirut. They began their explorations in Egypt, hoping to find the route of the Hebrew exodus. From there they went to Jerusalem via Aqaba and Hebron. They spent considerable time touring Judea. They then traveled to the north, visiting the areas of Nazareth and Tiberias. The trip took less than four months.

Robinson and Smith followed two basic principles as they conducted their research. (1) They stayed away from monasteries and their views regarding ancient sites. Rather, the two explorers depended primarily on the Bible and the native Arab population, the latter because Robinson recognized the importance of gathering modern place names in order to make correlations with ancient place names. (2) Robinson and Smith got off the beaten track in order to survey areas where few travelers had gone before (Moorey 1991, 16). Equipped with compass, telescope, thermometer, and measuring tape, the two men described their route to the smallest details, having measured distances, identified sites, and taken angle measurements of the more important finds.

Among the many achievements of Robinson and Smith was the first scientific survey of the Siloam tunnel in Jerusalem. They also found what later came to be called Robinson's Arch, a span supporting a stairway providing access to the temple mount during the time of Christ. Their discoveries were published as *Biblical Researches in Palestine and in the Adjacent Regions*. A second survey trip in 1852 was reported in the book *Later Biblical Researches*. So important were these studies that Swiss scholar Titus Tobler remarked in 1867, "The works of Robinson and Smith alone surpass the total of all previous contributions to Palestinian geography from the time of Eusebius and Jerome to the early nineteenth century." And according to Albrecht Alt (1939, 374), nearly all of Robinson's identifications of biblical sites and his topographical notes have stood the test of time; indeed, "in Robinson's footnotes are buried the errors of generations."

After Robinson's initial expedition "Palestine witnessed an unprecedented flood of western travelers intent on following in the footsteps of the learned American professor and recovering the splendor of the biblical past" (Silberman 1982, 51). Few of these travelers, however, worked systematically and professionally, and thus much of what they reported must be regarded as suspect. Most important was the American expedition to the Dead Sea in 1847–48. In a matter of three weeks, the team led by Lieutenant W. F. Lynch was able to chart the course of the Jordan River from the Sea of Galilee to the Dead Sea. In addition, they were able to collect a mass of scientific information about the Dead Sea itself. For example, they determined that the Dead Sea is the lowest point on the earth, lying

> **Hydrology:** *the study of water, its properties, sources, and distribution.*

1,300 feet below sea level. Lynch reported on the geography, geology, topography, hydrology, and zoology of the Dead Sea region.

Tobler visited Palestine for the purpose of scientific inquiry in 1845–46, 1858, and 1865. His first trip concentrated on Judea and produced a seven-volume study that consisted of 3,753 pages. He was the first to provide a detailed and clear description of the Church of the Holy Sepulchre in Jerusalem. He also examined many tombs in the valleys outside the holy city. His final visit focused on Nazareth and its environs. Although he contracted cholera there, he was able to produce a fundamental work about the region.

Victor Guérin, surveying Palestine from 1852 to 1875, covered in great detail Judea, Samaria, and Galilee. His studies were published in *Geography of Palestine*, which appeared during the years 1868–75. Guérin's work, however, was modest in its results: "he made relatively few identifications which have survived subsequent scrutiny" (Moorey 1991, 18). The fact is that Robinson had already done much of the work; as a result, "nothing was left for his successors but gleanings" (Albright 1949, 26).

Although this early phase consisted primarily of survey work, it was not devoid of excavation. In 1850–51 and 1863, Frédéric de Saulcy explored and excavated numerous sites in Palestine, such as the so-called Tombs of the Kings outside Jerusalem. Although his method of digging was primitive and he severely misdated the finds, William F. Albright declared him to be "the first modern excavator of a Palestinian site" (1949, 26). That designation may be improper, however, because "the first archaeological artifact ever discovered by excavation in Palestine" was unearthed by Lady Hester Lucy Stanhope in the early 1800s (Silberman 1982, 26). In either case, their work was little more than mere treasure-hunting. The excavations simply lacked expert care and scrutiny.

Although we owe a great debt to these pioneers of archaeology in Palestine, the results and value of their work were limited. Their "studies were mainly concerned with visible ruins related mostly to the Roman and later periods. The main achievement concerning the Old Testament period in this early phase of research was the identification of many biblical places with ruins and sites which in many cases preserved the ancient names" (Mazar 1990, 10–11). On the other hand, these individual pioneers did lay a solid foundation upon which later archaeological work might proceed.

Phase 2: Investigation by Society (1865—90)

The second period of archaeological inquiry was characterized by the establishment of learned societies dedicated to investigation of the ancient Near East. The first to be founded was the Palestine Exploration Fund. In November of 1865 this British organization sent its first expedition to Palestine under the leadership of Captain Charles Wilson. The chief objective of the team was to "locate such spots as might merit the further investigation of the Fund."

Although much of the archaeological work of this period continued to be survey, some important excavations did occur. Soon after the return of Wilson to London, the Palestine Exploration Fund sent another team to Palestine under the direction of Lieutenant Charles Warren. Its stated purpose was to excavate at the temple mount (Haram esh-Sharif) in Jerusalem (1867–70). Warren, however, was not allowed to excavate the mount itself. He did make some cuts outside the site. He concluded that the Haram esh-Sharif platform was the foundation of the temple of Herod from the New Testament period. Warren also dropped about thirty shafts in the areas immediately south and west of the mount. His team "succeeded in locating the southern and northern limits of the city, investigated an ancient subterranean aqueduct on the southern slope, and unearthed a number of pottery jar handles, stamped in ancient Hebrew with the words 'Belonging to the King,' which were the first genuine Biblical artifacts ever scientifically excavated in the Holy City" (Silberman 1982, 94).

In 1871 the Palestine Exploration Fund decided to undertake the daunting task of surveying and mapping the entire land of Palestine west of the Jordan River. The expedition was led by Lieutenant Claude Conder and Lieutenant H. H. Kitchener. Their survey work was completed in 1877. Published in four volumes in 1880, the survey covered approximately six thousand square miles. A large map was included (1 inch = 1 mile), and ten thousand names were recorded on it. The explorers reported to the fund that every site, ruin, and geographical feature of western Palestine had been dutifully recorded.

Survey work outside of western Palestine was also undertaken by the Palestine Exploration Fund. Most notably, Conder began a survey of Jordan (eastern Palestine) in 1881. He had finished about five hundred square miles of work when he was stopped by the Ottoman government. Conder published his findings under the title *The Survey of Eastern Palestine* (1889). Kitchener also did further surveying, providing (with Edward Hull) a complete geographical study of the Dead Sea region (1886).

The British were not the only ones active in Palestine during this phase. Established in 1870, the American Palestine Exploration Society sent John A. Paine to Palestine. He is best known for identifying the ancient site of Pisgah. The Germans were also operative with the founding of the Deutscher Palästina-Verein in 1877. Under the auspices of that society, Gottlieb Schumacher surveyed the Golan region east of the Sea of Galilee in 1884. The following year he continued his work to the south near the Yarmuk River. The French joined this archaeological march at a later date (1890) with the creation of the Ecole Biblique et Archéologique Française. Individual Frenchmen, such as Charles Clermont-Ganneau, had been in the field prior to this time, but most of the French working in Palestine had been sent by societies like the Palestine Exploration Fund.

Phase 3: Tell Excavation (1890–1914)

The modern era in the scientific study of archaeology in Palestine truly began in the year 1890. In that year William M. Flinders Petrie applied the groundbreaking work of Heinrich Schliemann at Troy to the archaeology of Palestine. Schliemann had discovered that the site of ancient Troy was a mound that represented a series of occupational layers, one lying on top of another. In general, each layer of the mound embodied a ruined city that had been built over a previously ruined city. Petrie appropriated this concept, called stratigraphy, and used it in his excavations at the Palestinian site of Tell el-Hesi. He discovered that each occupational layer of the mound had its own characteristic pottery. On that basis he argued that one could date the different levels of a site by the types of ceramic found therein. Some scholars, like Conder, were unconvinced of Petrie's methodology, but subsequent research and excavation have proven him to be correct (Albright 1949, 29).

Stratigraphy: *the study of the deposition and relationships of the occupational layers of an archaeological site.*

Petrie's methodology was revolutionary for the archaeology of Palestine. Although suggestions had been made by early travelers (such as Thomas Shaw some two hundred years before Petrie) that certain mounds might be artificial, most scholars of the nineteenth century worked under the assumption that they were merely natural hills. Robinson, Conder, and most of the early surveyors did their work on the basis of that premise. Petrie demonstrated that their surveys missed the most fundamental occupational sites of antiquity.

Soon after Petrie's discoveries, a flurry of excavations of Palestinian mounds took place. F. J. Bliss continued Petrie's work at Tell el-Hesi, and he published his four seasons of excavation in *A Mound of Many Cities* (1894). Bliss was able to confirm Petrie's theory of stratigraphy. This work was soon followed by digs at the mounds of Taanach (directed by Ernst Sellin, 1901–4), Jericho (Sellin and Carl Watzinger, 1907–9), Gezer (R. A. S. Macalister, 1902–9), Beth Shemesh (Duncan Mackenzie, 1911–12), Megiddo (Schumacher, 1903–5), and Samaria (D. G. Lyon and G. A. Reisner, 1908–10).

The initial period of tell excavation was formative for archaeology in Palestine today. "The foundations of the discipline were laid in the first appreciation of the true nature of the tell and how it was formed. Archaeologists began to learn how to disentangle the successive strata and to date each by its contents, particularly the pottery. . . . The result was that by 1914 a rough outline of the history and culture of ancient Palestine had been produced" (Dever 1980, 42).

Much is owed to the pioneers of mound excavation. By today's standards, however, their excavation principles and techniques were quite primitive. For the most part, stratigraphy was neglected by the early excavators. In addition, "surveying and levelling were utterly inadequate; the architectural aspects of the dig were dealt with only sketchily" (Albright 1949, 31). Pottery as a chronological indicator was only sporadically used. Schumacher's work at Megiddo is a case in point. It is almost useless for the archaeologist today because of its poor stratigraphic technique and limited use of dating by means of ceramic.

A final aspect of the development of archaeology at the turn to the twentieth century was the establishment of foreign archaeological institutions in Jerusalem. The German Evangelical School was founded in 1902 under the direction of Albrecht Alt, the British School of Archaeology in 1919, the Ecole Biblique in 1890, and the American School of Oriental Research in 1900. Their purpose was to foster surveys and excavations in Palestine. Typical was the American School's resolution "to enable properly qualified persons to prosecute Biblical, linguistic, archaeological, historical, and other kindred studies and researches under more favorable conditions than can be secured at a distance from the Holy Land" (King 1983, 27).

Phase 4: Systematic Archaeology (1918–40)

Between the world wars, archaeology in Palestine came of age. It jettisoned, for the most part, any image it had of mere treasure-hunting. The field now developed sophisticated techniques and methodology, as well as scholarly competence (Dever 1980, 43). The outline of the chronology of ancient Palestine came into clear focus and basically remains the same today. Scholars today deal largely with mere details. Most importantly, the academicians of phase 4 began to see how Palestine fit into the rest of the ancient Near East, both culturally and physically. Because of this period's many advances, it has sometimes been referred to as the golden age of biblical archaeology (Moorey 1991, 54).

Much of the movement toward a more systematic, scientific type of archaeology was due to the work of C. S. Fisher. From 1925 until his death in 1941 he served as professor of archaeology at the American School in Jerusalem. Fisher opened the major excavations at Beth Shean (1921), Megiddo (1925), and Beth Shemesh (1928). His most lasting contribution, however, was the development of systematic excavation techniques and a detailed recording system. In fact, throughout this phase Fisher's methodology was employed by most archaeologists in Palestine.

Locus: *a specific area of work at an excavation site.*

The Megiddo excavations begun by Fisher were later taken over by P. L. O. Guy (1927). Guy helped to improve the control that an archaeologist has by assigning locus numbers to the specific areas being excavated and by employing aerial photography. He was followed by Gordon Loud, who brought to publication many of the finds at Megiddo. His report was a landmark, as he included complete sets of plans for each stratum of the site; *Megiddo II* is yet a standard work in the field.

Although Fisher was more well known at the time, it was William F. Albright who had the greatest impact upon later archaeology in Palestine. G. Ernest Wright accurately comments, "It must be said that Albright created the discipline of Palestinian archaeology as we know it" (1970, 27). Albright began excavations at the site of Tell Beit Mirsim in 1926. There he mastered the crafts of ceramic typology and stratigraphic analysis. The chronology of the Bronze and Iron Ages that he ascertained through these excavations remains the standard for today's archaeologists. Indeed, Albright's work at Tell Beit Mirsim "marked such a significant step in the development of ceramic chronology that even today no student of Syro-Palestinian archaeology can afford to neglect the Tell Beit Mirsim publications" (King 1975, 60). Albright's influence upon archaeology in Palestine was staggering. The work of scholars such as Wright, Nelson Glueck, and their students owed much to his pioneering efforts.

Jewish archaeologists from Palestine became active during this phase (Albright 1970). Excavations directed by Benjamin Mazar, E. L. Sukenik, Michael Avi-Yonah, Nahman Avigad, and others were important contributions to the discipline. In addition, they provided the foundation and impetus for the later Israeli school of archaeologists that would appear in the late 1940s and early 1950s (Meyers 1987).

So many excavations occurred in Palestine during this period that we can mention only a few. The reader should consider the digs at Bethel (1934), Tell en-Nasbeh (1926–35), Jericho (1929–36), and Samaria (1931–35). The archaeology of Palestine developed in other spheres as well. For example, in 1929 John D. Rockefeller Jr. donated one million dollars for the express purpose of constructing the Palestine Archaeological Museum in Jerusalem. In addition, archaeological publications multiplied, with the printing of such journals as the *Biblical Archaeologist* and the *Bulletin of the American Schools of Oriental Research*.

Phase 5: A Methodological Revolution (1948–67)

Between the beginning of World War II and the Israeli War of Independence (1948) little archaeological work was accomplished. The political and military environment was too hostile and volatile. After the partitioning of the land of Palestine and the

founding of the nation of Israel, however, archaeology greatly pros-
pered and thrived.

The principal development of the period took place at the excavations of Jericho (1952–58) and Jerusalem (1961–67) under the
direction of the British archaeologist Kathleen Kenyon. At these
two sites Kenyon introduced the British archaeological methods
of Mortimer Wheeler to the digging in Palestine: "Here she dug in
smaller squares (usually 5 x 5 m) within a grid, leaving interven-
ing catwalks, or 'balks,' which were then used to see the debris in
section and to guide careful probing and stripping of the debris"
(Dever 1980, 44).

Kenyon's technique stressed the stratification of the site.
Prior to her work, archaeologists utilized the architectural
method, which aimed at wide-scale exposure of complete buildings (Ussishken 1982, 94). The consequences of what has come
to be known as the Wheeler-Kenyon method were revolutionary. The leaving of a balk, for example, provided a third dimension in an excavation area. That component allowed the
archaeologist to view what had been excavated, and to see how
the current level of excavation compared with what went
before. This methodology also gave a great element of control
over the excavation area.

The two types of excavation systems, the architectural method
and the Wheeler-Kenyon method, vied for the hearts of archaeologists during this period. Americans who were digging at
Shechem (1956–66) under Wright's direction embraced
Kenyon's technique. They coupled it with the traditional attention that American archaeologists gave to pottery analysis. The
Shechem excavation served as a classroom for a generation of
American diggers, and many of them today retain its two
emphases.

Israeli archaeologists began to contribute greatly to the discipline at this time. The excavation of Hazor by Yigael Yadin was a
salient event (1955–58). This dig was a workshop for a generation
of Israeli archaeologists, including Yohanan Aharoni, Ruth Amiran, and Moshe and Trude Dothan. The tendency of this school
was to use an architectural approach to excavation. While this
method freed the archaeologists to expose vast areas of architecture, some stratigraphic control was lost. The issue of excavation

technique dominated the literature of the time. It was a perplexing question, one that would not be solved until the next phase of archaeology in Palestine.

Phase 6: New Horizons (1967–)

Current field work in Palestine employs a method that combines both the Wheeler-Kenyon system and the architectural approach. "As much as possible of the area of the site is exposed with the intention of uncovering complete architectural units and studying their layout. Cross-examination of the occupational history is achieved by excavating at several different points. Analysis of the earth layers is not neglected: sections are examined and in many cases recorded by drawing and photography" (Mazar 1990, 25). The compromise between the two methods has provided a good balance in excavation.

One major innovation in the discipline over the last thirty years is the multidisciplinary approach. It is very common for digs to employ osteologists, botanists, geologists, zoologists, and other specialists. They can contribute from their field of expertise to the understanding of the material culture of a site. The excavations at Gezer (1964–73) under Wright, William G. Dever, and Joe D. Seger were the first in Palestine to involve multicultural studies. Gezer was also the site of the first field-school, the dig serving as an outdoor classroom for students. Many of today's American archaeologists were trained at Gezer. The multicultural approach adopted there was soon emulated by the excavations at Beersheba (1969–75), Tell el-Hesi (1970–), Caesarea (1971–), Lachish (1972–), and Ashkelon (1985–).

> Regional archaeology: *the study of the material remains of a geographical area that covers numerous sites.*

Recent years have also seen cooperation between archaeologists from different countries. Joint projects between Israeli and American scholars are common. For example, the excavation at Tell Michal was directed by Ze'ev Herzog of Tel Aviv University and James Muhly of the University of Pennsylvania (1977–80).

Another direction of current archaeology is the regional approach. That is, archaeologists study not only a mound but also its surroundings and environment. This approach provides a comprehensive archaeological context for the site being excavated. Only then can a proper picture of settlement be achieved. It is likely that the regional approach began with Aharoni's work at Beersheba (Ussishken 1982, 95).

Finally, archaeology in Palestine is more extensive and challenging today than it used to be. Many types of excavations occur nowadays. Not only are tells dug, but many small-scale excavations are undertaken. Salvage excavation is occurring at an unprecedented rate. Major surveys of the land continue. This has all led to information explosion. How the discipline of archaeology will deal with it is a question yet to be resolved.

Where Does Archaeology Go from Here?

Although archaeology in Palestine continues to progress and dozens of excavations are in process, the discipline has some serious problems. Spiraling expenses are one major factor. One season of a large dig can cost hundreds of thousands of dollars. Sources for that amount of money are limited, and thus the competition for it is fierce. Another issue is that many archaeologists have failed to publish their findings. There are many reasons for this neglect. However, it only hinders efforts to gain a proper picture of the culture of ancient Palestine. Such problems at times seem almost insurmountable.

No greater dilemma exists, however, than the question of motivation for excavation in Palestine. What is the purpose of excavation in Palestine? What impact ought religion have upon archaeology? What influence should the scientific approach have? What about the place of biblical studies?

On the one side of the issue stand those who favor a distinct separation between biblical studies and archaeological research. It is their opinion that the link between the two is largely artificial. Those who attempt to integrate the two fields are guilty of trying to prove the Bible. Archaeology for too long has been the weak sister of biblical research. It is time that archaeology stand apart and take its place as a scientific discipline, no longer under the shadow of biblical studies.

On the other side of the issue are those who insist that biblical scholars ought to be involved in archaeology. Historically, archaeology has been the work of biblical scholars, such as Albright, Glueck, and Wright. These men did not sacrifice science, but made important scientific contributions even though their main field was biblical studies. In addition, it is only natural that the two disciplines work hand in hand because they are a source of knowledge and discovery for one another. It is not our place to provide a solution to this problem. But we want the reader to be aware of the controversy since it may have a great impact on the future of archaeology as we know it.

Bibliography

Albright, W. F. 1949. *The Archaeology of Palestine*. Harmondsworth, Eng.: Penguin.

———. 1970. "The Phenomenon of Israeli Archaeology." In *Near Eastern Archaeology in the Twentieth Century*, ed. J. A. Sanders, 57–63. Garden City, N.Y.: Doubleday.

Alt, A. 1939. "Edward Robinson and the Historical Geography of Palestine." *JBL* 58:373–77.

Biblical Archaeology Today, 1990: Proceedings of the Second International Congress on Biblical Archaeology. 1993. Jerusalem: Israel Exploration Society.

Dever, W. G. 1980. "Archaeological Method in Israel: A Continuing Revolution." *BA* 43.1:40–48.

———. 1992. "Archaeology, Syro-Palestinian and Biblical." *ABD* 1:354–67.

King, P. J. 1975. "The American Archaeological Heritage in the Near East." *BASOR* 217:55–65.

———. 1983. *American Archaeology in the Mideast: A History of the American Schools of Oriental Research*. Philadelphia: ASOR.

Mazar, A. 1990. *Archaeology of the Land of the Bible*. New York: Doubleday.

Meyers, E. M. 1987. "Judaic Studies and Archaeology: The Rochaeology: The Legacy of M. Avi-Yonah." *EI* 19:21–27.

Moorey, P. R. S. 1991. *A Century of Biblical Archaeology*. Louisville: Westminster John Knox.

Robinson, E. 1856. *Biblical Researches in Palestine*. 3 vols. Boston: Crocker and Brewster.

Silberman, N. A. 1982. *Digging for God and Country: Exploration, Archeology, and the Secret Struggle for the Holy Land*. New York: Knopf.

Stern, E., ed. 1993. *The New Encyclopedia of Archaeological Excavations in the Holy Land*. 4 vols. New York: Simon and Schuster.

Ussishken, D. 1982. "Where Is Israeli Archaeology Going?" *BA* 45.2:93–95.

Wright, G. E. 1970. "The Phenomenon of American Archaeology." In *Near Eastern Archaeology in the Twentieth Century*, ed. J. A. Sanders, 3–40. Garden City, N.Y.: Doubleday.

The Tales of Tells 3

Indiana Jones brushing away some sand to discover an Egyptian temple or finding a valuable artifact after dodging a maze of booby traps (and, of course, winning the blonde!) is the image many people have when they think of archaeology. Others, who have witnessed excavations in the West, picture digs at Indian sites or colonial towns and houses, such as George Washington's home at Valley Forge. Most of them are characterized as one-period sites, that is, the time of occupation can be measured in decades. These settlements are normally quite small as well. For these reasons, the archaeologist in the West is required to use diminutive tools of excavation, like the dental pick and brush. The material remains at a site commonly tell about one group at one time in history, and thus, cultural continuity dominates archaeology in the West.

Doing Archaeology in the Land of the Bible is much different. Excavation in the Middle East rarely deals with one-period sites; rather, it focuses on towns, villages, and cities that have been repeatedly occupied for hundreds and even thousands of years. For example, the site of Megiddo in the Jezreel Valley was first inhabited in the Neolithic period (c. 5000 B.C.) and last settled in the Persian period of the fifth and fourth centuries B.C. Obviously, there were many occupations between its founding and its final destruction, particularly during the Chalcolithic, Early Bronze, Middle Bronze, Late Bronze, and Iron Ages. Megiddo had a 4,500-year settlement history. As a further example, the Shephelah town of Tell el-Hesi was originally built in the Early Bronze Age (c. 3000 B.C.); its final stage was probably as a military outpost in the twentieth century A.D. (Shell casings were discovered on top of the site.) The cultural continuity between the various occupations at a site was minimal: different peoples with different material cultures settled the site at different times in history. For instance, the Iron Age inhabitants of Megiddo built houses, made pottery, and fortified the town in ways distinct from those of Megiddo's Early Bronze Age residents. If, as is not unusual, the archaeologist uncovers fifteen to twenty occupation levels of a site, a great variety of material remains will be present.

This is not the Indiana Jones perspective on archaeology, nor does it much reflect archaeology in the West. But, frankly, it is no less interesting. This chapter will explain the pattern of settlements in the ancient Near East.

The Mound

In ancient times a group looking for a place to settle would be drawn to a particular site for a variety of reasons. Perhaps the most important prerequisite for an ancient settlement was a permanent water source. Before the invention of cisterns and aqueducts, towns were built near wells, springs, or streams. Early settlements were, therefore, found only in limited areas in which perennial water sources existed. Not surprisingly, the earliest human habitation in Palestine was in the Jordan River Valley and in the region of the Sea of Galilee.

Availability of rich agricultural land and other natural resources was another important factor (Borowski 1981). Although farming would serve as the primary economic base of the first community at a site, sustenance could also be partially provided by commerce. Trade routes, therefore, were of great value to an emerging settlement (Pritchard 1967).

Defense was another crucial consideration in initial settlement. Many Palestinian towns were first located on rocky outcrops because the height provided a good defensive position (Lapp 1975, 1–3). Elevation also gave the settlement an advantage in controlling the all-important commercial thoroughfares that passed by. Some have suggested that elevation also provided protection against flood waters (LaSor 1979, 237). Thus the settling of Palestinian sites was different from what occurred in Mesopotamia, where villages were erected directly at ground level. City fortifications first appeared in Palestine during the Neolithic period; from that time on, walls, towers, and gates were erected on top of the rocky outcrops. The combination of a natural mound and man-made defense systems made the Palestinian settlement quite secure.

The pioneers of an area usually erected their town on a natural mound. They constructed houses, public buildings, streets, silos, wells, and, as already mentioned, gates and city walls. The materials used in building were either mud-brick or stone, or a combination of the two. Mud-brick is sun-dried clay that usually includes some sort of binding element like straw, palm-tree fibers, bones, or seashells (Glueck 1940). When mud-brick is properly formed, dried thoroughly, and skillfully laid, it may last for centuries. In addition to endurance, mud-brick has the advantage of flexibility: it withstands natural disasters like earthquakes very well. Torrential rains appear to have little adverse impact on mud-brick constructions. Fortification walls of mud-brick provide especially good protection because they are so resilient. They have some give, and siege machines thus have a difficult time knocking them down.

Even so, ancient cities, towns, and villages did not last forever. They were destroyed in one way or another. War was a major cause of destruction. Natural disasters like drought, earthquake, and fire could also decimate a settlement. Disease (pestilence and plague) could ravage the population and lead to abandonment of a town. Natural decay and neglect also could take their toll and make rebuilding necessary. In ancient Palestine some cities underwent numerous large-scale rebuildings. For whatever reason, almost every ancient site eventually became unoccupied.

After a site was destroyed or abandoned, natural elements came into play. The prevailing west winds of Palestine, seasonal rains (sometimes torrential), and drifting sands speeded the decay (Albright 1949, 17). These natural elements caused erosion down the sides of the mound, and debris filled in the low-lying spots. After decades, or even a century or two, the deterioration of the remains of human habitation would be quite drastic and dramatic.

In ancient Palestine new settlers tended to occupy and rebuild previously inhabited sites. Their reasons were the same as those of the original occupants: water, trade, and defense. The newcomers would not remove the ruins of the previous occupation, but would

Figure 2

Vertical Section of a Small Tell

(Adapted and reproduced from *The Old Testament and the Archaeologist*
by H. Darrell Lance, copyright © 1981 Fortress Press. Used by permission of Augsburg Fortress.)

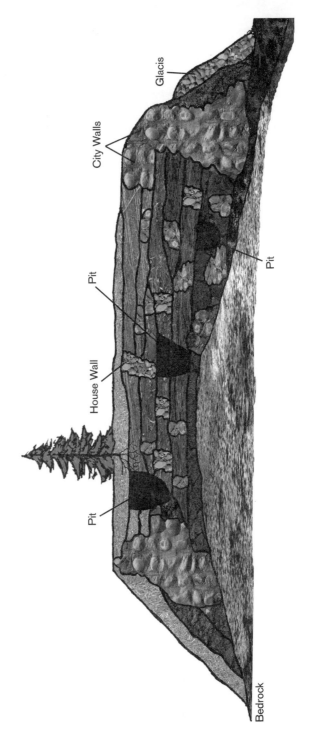

build directly on top of them. That practice enhanced some of the assets of the site. First of all, defense would improve because the new city would be erected on higher ground. The depth of debris on which the new settlement was built varied from a few inches to many feet (Kenyon 1970, 30). In any event, almost

> Stratum: *a layer of earth containing the remains of a single period of occupation during which there was no major gap in architecture or culture.*

every mound in ancient Palestine rose higher with each subsequent occupation. Second, the walls remaining from the earlier occupation made rebuilding much easier. Fallen stone walls provided some building material for subsequent cities. In addition, when fortification walls were built on top of previous walls, the defensive position of the site improved.

After a period of habitation the second settlement was also destroyed. A third settlement usually followed. The cycle of settlement–destruction–vacancy–new settlement could be repeated several times over the course of a mound's history. Megiddo, for example, contained over twenty occupational levels.

Each successive occupation layer of a mound is called a stratum (pl. strata). A series of strata, one on top of another, results in a mound looking like "a low truncated cone, with flat top and sloping sides" (Albright 1949, 16).[1] This form has often been compared to a cake with many layers.

The most peculiar physical feature of the mound is its flat top. After the final habitation and destruction, natural elements helped cover the mound with debris. The external walls of the ancient city held much of the

> Glacis: *a long fortification slope running from the bottom of a mound to the defensive wall on top.*

debris in place and prevented erosion to some degree. Over time, the surface debris gave a flat definition to the mound (Free 1992, 16–17).

The steep sloping configuration of the mound usually resulted from the building of a glacis around the town. A fortification slope made of layers of rubble that ran from the top of a defensive rampart to ground level, the glacis usually encircled the entire mound. Acting much like a girdle, it served to disallow erosion and thus held the mound together. Consequently, the sides of the occupation mound were much steeper than a natural hill (Borowski 1981). And so, as the man-made mound grew higher with each occupation, the area for building lessened. Thus the mound took on its peculiar cone shape.

In Palestine a stratified mound is called a tell.[2] That term perhaps derived from Akkadian *sillu* or Sumerian *dul*, both of which meant "mound; heap of ruins; female breast." The word is used several times in the Bible to refer to cities which were built on top of one another. For example, Joshua 11:13 reads: "Israel did not burn any cities that stood on their mounds [pl. of Hebrew *tel*] except Hazor alone, which Joshua burned."[3] And in Jeremiah 30:18 the prophet promises a glorious return from the exile for the people of God: "Thus says the LORD, 'Behold, I will restore the fortunes of the tents of Jacob, and have compassion on his dwellings; the city shall be rebuilt upon its mound [Hebrew *tel*]'" (RSV).

> Tell: *a mound consisting of debris from cities built on top of one another on the same site.*

The landscape of the Middle East is dotted with tells. Nelson Glueck, for instance, charted well over two hundred ancient mounds in the Jordan Valley between the Yarmuk and Jabbok Rivers, a distance of a mere thirty miles. More-recent surveys have discovered some sites that Glueck had overlooked. Most pre-Hellenistic towns in ancient Palestine were erected on mounds. Certainly other types of ancient settlements are known—such as prehistoric cave dwellings and seminomadic encampments—but the fact remains, most people in ancient Palestine lived on tells.

The size of tells in Palestine is not uniform. The largest mound is Hazor, north of the Sea of Galilee. It occupies about 190 acres. Many diminutive tells cover only a slim half-acre of ground. Estimates of the average size of a tell in Palestine run anywhere from 7 to 20 acres (Mazar 1990, 9). Actually tells in Palestine are quite small in comparison to those in the rest of the Near East. Nippur, a Mesopotamian city, was built on three tells covering about 370 acres. Thus it was twice as big as the largest tell in Palestine. Nineveh was erected on twin tells which had a circumference of 7.75 miles! Although much smaller than their counterparts in Mesopotamia, the Palestinian mounds were the most significant and most common type of settlement in that area during antiquity.

Discovery of the Tell

For the greater part of the nineteenth century, the nature of tells and stratigraphy remained a mystery. When the great pioneer Edward Robinson first visited the site of Tell el-Hesi in the 1830s he remarked: "The form of the Tell is singular, a truncated cone with a fine plain on the top. . . . From the information of our guides, and from the remarkable appearance of this isolated Tell, we had expected to find here traces of ruins. . . . Yet we could discover nothing whatever to mark the existence of any former town or structure" (Robinson 1841, 390; Moorey 1981, 21).

Not until 1870, when Heinrich Schliemann (1822–90) excavated Troy, which is located in modern Turkey, was the conclusion drawn that a tell is accumulated layers of deposit.[4] He was the first to excavate a tell with the understanding that it was one ruined city overlying another. Twenty years later an eccentric Englishman applied Schliemann's discovery to the land of Palestine.

In 1890 an excavation took place at the site of Tell el-Hesi, a thirty-four-acre mound in southern Palestine. The archaeologist of Hesi was a man named William M. Flinders Petrie (1853–1942). Petrie, an Egyptologist by profession, had been in the Middle East since 1880 when he came to Egypt to measure and study the great pyramids at Giza. Because of unstable conditions in Egypt at the end of that decade, Petrie thought it prudent to leave the country. The British Palestine Exploration Fund immediately appointed him to direct the first archaeological excavation in Palestine. Petrie arrived at Tell el-Hesi in the spring of 1890 and conducted a six-week excavation.

Petrie endured many trials and dangers at Hesi. Living conditions were wretched. He slept in a tent, ate local food, drank local water, and spent much of his time being sick. He had little companionship because all his workers were Arabs who kept to themselves. His only transportation was by horse or camel, and any suitable place of habitation was two to three days away. He also had the problem of not being able to dig on the top of the mound because it was under cultivation by a local farmer! But despite the hardships Petrie achieved his goal. In his own words, "I had six weeks of work there, including the whole month of Ramadan, when work is very difficult for the fasting and thirsty Muslims. But in that time, and without disturbing the crops, I succeeded in unravelling the history of the place."

What Petrie did was to cut vertical sections into the slopes of the mound. By probing the tell in that manner, he uncovered sixty feet of superimposed occupation, one layer blanketing another. He determined that there had been eleven cities during the history of Tell el-Hesi, spanning a period of approximately three thousand years. When one city was destroyed, another city was built right on top of it.

The basic principle of stratigraphy is the backbone of modern archaeology: a tell is an accumulation of one ruined city on top of another, and what is at the bottom of the mound must be earlier in date than what is at the top (Franken and Franken-Battershill 1963, 6). Every excavation of a mound in Israel bases its research and findings on the method that Petrie introduced to Palestine. His work ushered in a golden age of archaeological excavation in Israel. As a result of his success at Hesi, large expeditions were quickly funded to explore many ancient Israelite sites, such as Megiddo, Jericho, Gezer, and Samaria. Accordingly, the groundbreaking work at Tell el-Hesi earned Petrie the title the Father of Palestinian Archaeology.

The Difficulties in Tell Investigation

Although the development of a tell appears to be straightforward, in reality its configuration is the result of fairly complicated processes. The sequence of deposits, structures, and debris is quite irregular. Thus an occupation layer is by no means laid out evenly across a mound, nor are its remains found at a uniform depth. As a result, the stratigraphy of a tell can be extremely complex. The irregularities of mound deposition are due to various factors, a few of which we will consider. (For a fuller treatment see Kenyon 1971; Blakely and Toombs 1981; Dever and Lance 1978; Lance 1981.)

Pits. At almost every tell excavated in Palestine, archaeologists have found an extraordinary number of pits. They were usually constructed after one of two standard designs: the bell shape and the cylinder shape. A variant of the latter is the bottle shape: a small opening and a narrow neck lead to a larger body or cavity.

Figure 3
Cylindrical and Bell-Shaped Pits from the Agricultural Project at Lahav

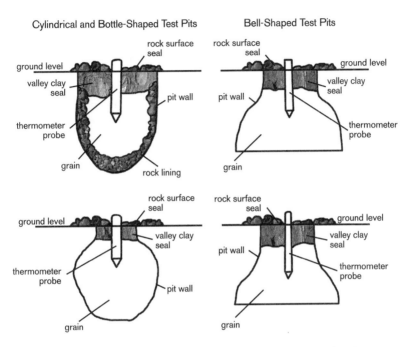

The cylindrical pit can reach a width of ten feet and a depth of sixteen feet. The bell-shaped pit sometimes measures up to eight feet wide and twelve feet deep.

These pits were dug for a variety of reasons. For one, new settlers searched for building materials from earlier periods to use in their own construction. These man-made depressions are sometimes referred to as "robber pits." Other pits were used as latrines, cooking ovens, facilities for making compost, refuse containers, and cisterns (Currid and Gregg 1988). Most pits on mounds were probably used for grain storage, a point confirmed by recent testing at Lahav (Tell Halif) (Currid and Navon 1989).

> Robber pits/trenches: *depressions dug by new settlers who removed stones from earlier structures for use in their own building projects.*

Pits cause major problems in stratigraphic analysis because they cut into earlier strata. Not only was the digging intrusive, but it also destroyed earlier material. And if the purpose was to obtain building materials, another problem emerges: earlier building materials and styles may be found in later architecture. Such is the case at Caesarea where Crusader builders erected a castle that combined Herodian building blocks with their own construction techniques and stone. Clearly, pits can wreak havoc on the stratigraphy of a site.[5]

Fills. Between occupation strata on a tell are various levels of debris called fills. Some of these occurred naturally, but often debris was brought in to level an uneven area for future building (Wright 1962a, 34). A fill may pose a major problem in analyzing stratigraphy because the debris may have been taken from another part of the mound that predates the stratum upon which it was then deposited as filler material. Say, for example, that a Middle Bronze Age occupation had been destroyed, and a group from the Late Bronze Age decided to build a new town directly on its ruins. The Late Bronze settlers, however, found that part of the tell was too irregular to build upon, so they dug elsewhere on the mound to get debris for leveling the surface. This filler dirt contained pottery and other objects from the Early Bronze Age. Once the debris had been deposited by the Late Bronze builders, the Early Bronze materials would lie on top of Middle Bronze remains. This primitive form of bulldozing can be a hazard to the archaeologist attempting to uncover the history of a tell.

Fill: *a level of debris brought into a site to level an area for new construction.*

Foundation trenches. Another problem that an archaeologist faces when trying to determine the sequence of strata is the foundation trench. When ancient builders constructed a wall, they usually inserted its footing or base into a trench that was dug into earlier levels. The excavator needs to be careful to identify the materials in the trench as part of the wall and not of earlier strata. Contamination of materials from the foundation trench with contiguous levels must be avoided at all costs (Blakely and Toombs 1981, 22).

Foundation trench: *a ditch dug by ancient builders for the foundation of a wall.*

Wash. The force of water, for example, from torrential rains, may create wash layers. These are layers of debris that have been moved by water from one part of a tell and deposited in another. As a result, the debris, pottery, and other remains from different occupation levels are intermixed. Such intermixing is especially common on slopes that are susceptible to erosion.

Tombs. Certain groups buried their dead on top of a tell. At Tell el-Hesi, for example, numerous Muslim burials were discovered in a late occupation layer of the mound. The problem for stratigraphy is the same as that presented by pits: burials intrude into earlier levels of habitation. They are holes that ancient people scooped out of earlier material for their own use. The archaeologist must not confuse the burial remains with the findings in the abutting strata because they most likely come from different periods. By dismissing caution when excavating tombs, valuable evidence can be misrepresented.

Rebuilding. A tell was formed by the construction of one city on top of another. This rebuilding took on different forms in ancient Palestine. Sometimes, as mentioned before, fill was brought in to provide a foundation for new building. But, occasionally, strata were removed to provide a level surface for construction. The removal of strata in one part of a mound but not in another results in different stratigraphic sequences. Excavators must be acutely aware of such building practices.

Some tells were expanded by rebuilding, although this was accomplished only with great difficulty. Hazor is a good example. At the end of the Middle Bronze Age, builders made the town six times as large as the original tell. They dug a defensive moat and then used the dirt as a fill to erect a platform with a defensive wall on top (Lapp 1975, 2). Around the same time, a great fill at Shechem was incorporated within an enlarged city wall. Such expansions were not common, but the archaeologist must not be taken by surprise when they do appear.

What a tell is and how it was formed should be clear by now. Also evident is that each tell has its own identity and occupational history. Some sites had a long and complicated development: the tell of Beth Shean, for instance, has over seventy feet of occupational debris. The stratigraphy of such a tell may be very complex, with pits, fills, washes, and rebuilding, so that the history of the site is difficult to determine. Other sites are small forts that have only one occupational stratum, in which case the history is easy to uncover. In any event, each tell tells its own tale. No two tells are the same. The task of the archaeologist is to dig up the story that is hidden in the mound.

Bibliography

Albright, W. F. 1949. *The Archaeology of Palestine*. Harmondsworth, Eng.: Penguin.

Blakely, J. A., and L. E. Toombs. 1981. *The Tell el-Hesi Field Manual*. Winona Lake, Ind.: Eisenbrauns.

Borowski, O. 1981. "How to Tell a Tell." *BAR* 7.2:66–67.

Cole, C. 1977. "How a Dig Begins." *BAR* 3.2:32–36.

Currid, J., and J. Gregg. 1988. "Why Did the Early Israelites Dig All Those Pits?" *BAR* 14.5:54–57.

Currid, J., and A. Navon. 1989. "Iron Age Pits and the Lahav (Tell Halif) Grain Storage Project." *BASOR* 273:67–78.

Dever, W. G., and H. D. Lance, eds. 1978. *A Manual of Field Excavation: Handbook for Field Archaeologists*. Cincinnati: Hebrew Union College.

Franken, H. J., and C. A. Franken-Battershill. 1963. *A Primer of Old Testament Archaeology*. Leiden: Brill.

Free, J. P. 1992. *Archaeology and Bible History*. Grand Rapids: Zondervan.

Glueck, N. 1940. "Ezion-Geber: Elath—City of Bricks with Straw." *BA* 3.4:51–55.

Kenyon, K. 1957. *Digging Up Jericho*. New York: Praeger.

———. 1970. *Archaeology in the Holy Land*. 3d ed. New York: Praeger.

———. 1971. "An Essay on Archaeological Technique: The Publication of Results from the Excavation of a Tell." *HTR* 64:271–79.

Lance, H. D. 1981. *The Old Testament and the Archaeologist*. Philadelphia: Fortress.

Lapp, P. 1975. *The Tale of the Tell*. Pittsburgh: Pickwick.

LaSor, W. S. 1979. "Archeology." In *International Standard Bible Encyclopedia*, ed. G. W. Bromiley, 1:235–44. Grand Rapids: Eerdmans.

Mazar, A. 1990. *Archaeology of the Land of the Bible*. New York: Doubleday.

Moorey, P. R. S. 1981. *Excavation in Palestine*. Guildford, Eng.: Lutterworth.

Pritchard, J. 1967. "Introduction." In *Archaeological Discoveries in the Holy Land*, compiled by the Archaeological Institute of America, xii–xiii. New York: Bonanza.

Robinson, E. 1841. *Biblical Researches in Palestine II*. London: J. Murray.

Stiebing, W. H., Jr. 1981. "Who First Excavated Stratigraphically?" *BAR* 7.1:52–53.

Wright, G. E. 1962a. "Archaeological Fills and Strata." *BA* 25.2:34–40.

———. 1962b. *Biblical Archaeology*. Philadelphia: Westminster.

1. In the background, the tell at Beth Shean; it is 262.5 feet high with eighteen superimposed layers. In the foreground are the remains of the Roman city.

2. Student volunteer using a handpick to clear debris from a stone wall.

3. A typical excavation square.

4. An excavation trench dug at Megiddo by the University of Chicago in the 1930s.

5. A common Israelite four-room house at Beersheba (the author is explaining the structure).

6. An early Bronze high place (altar) at Megiddo.

7. Foundations of the Solomonic gateway at Megiddo.

8. Mud-brick atop a stone foundation (gateway at Beersheba).

9. A tripartite pillared building at Hazor; it probably served as a storehouse.

10. Tripartite pillared buildings at Beersheba; piles of pottery were stored in some of the rooms.

11. An example of mud-brick construction at Beersheba. Note the straw that served as temper for the bricks.

12. A mud-brick four-room house at Beersheba. The back wall of the house also functioned as part of the outer wall of the city.

13. An example of a wall with a stone base and a mud-brick superstructure (a four-room house at Beersheba).

14. A fieldstone wall at Megiddo.

15. Basalt stone construction at Chorazin in Galilee.

16. An offset-inset wall at Arad from the period of the kings of Judah.

17. Roman building techniques as used at Herodian Jericho: opus reticulatum (small square stones set at a 45° angle) and opus quadratum (brick-shaped stones laid horizontally).

18. Lower courses of the temple mount in Jerusalem; the large cut rocks with incised marginal drafting are typical of Herodian stone masonry.

19. Cave 4 at Qumran; the Dead Sea Scrolls, probably the greatest small find ever, were found here and in other caves in the area.

20. A capital at Capernaum with a carved replica of the ark of the covenant.

21. An elongated room of a storehouse from the Roman remains at Masada.

22. Synagogue remains from Masada; below the black line on the back wall is what archaeologists found in situ; above it is modern reconstruction.

23. The Early Bronze city of Arad; note the outer fortification wall with its projecting towers.

24. A cylindrical pit from the agricultural project at Lahav; see figure 3 (p. 45).

25. Carved basalt capital on top of a column in the synagogue at Chorazin.

26. Heart-shaped column in the synagogue at Capernaum.

Living by Site (Surveying) 4

Does an archaeologist have any clues regarding what remains are at a tell before excavation? Or does one excavate blindly? Actual digging is only a part, albeit a large part, of archaeological field-work. In reality, much work that can reveal information about a mound, its history, and its surroundings can be done before digging. There are many ways to gather such data, like studying the Bible or other ancient writings that mention the site or region. The most frequently used method is the archaeological survey, which may be defined as "the work of discovering attributes of human cultures from the features and artifacts that lie exposed on the surface" (Kautz 1988, 209). A preliminary work to excavation, surveying has the important purpose of previewing what lies below in the tell. This chapter will briefly present the techniques, the goals, the limitations, and an example of surveys and their value to archaeological study.

Surveying Methods

For the most part, archaeological surveys in Israel fall into two categories: examination of individual sites and analysis of regions.[1] For the purposes of surveys in the first category "any significant artifacts in close proximity to one another would be designated a site. Thus a site could be as small as a single, fragmented milestone, or as large as a major *tell*" (Ibach 1976, 119). In the survey of tells, the field techniques espoused by Charles Redman and Patty J. Watson (1970) have been widely employed. Their method was put into practice, for example, at the tell of Jalul in central Jordan (Ibach 1978).

The first step taken at Jalul was the drawing of a contour map of the tell. A 10-meter grid was then superimposed on the map, and "one 10 m. x 10 m. square in each block of nine was chosen by means of a random-numbers table. The result was a selection of 101 squares scattered over the top and slopes of the *tell* and down to the plain as far as sherd density remained substantial" (Ibach 1978, 217). One-ninth of the mound, or 10,100 square meters, was thus set apart for surveying.

Contour/grid map: *a plan showing the shape of the land surface and the areas to be excavated.*

Each randomly selected square was marked off by stakes and string. The surveyors then systematically walked through each square, picking up every pottery sherd larger than a thumbnail. Every piece of pottery was dated, recorded, and described. In this manner the archaeologists were able to date the various layers of the Jalul tell. This survey thus provided some useful information about what remains might be expected during excavation.

A regional survey uses methods other than those used at a single site (Kautz 1981). This type of survey begins by searching for and locating ancient sites (Alon and Levy 1980, 140–41). Their locations are plotted on a regional map that has a standard grid. This work is then collated with earlier surveys and maps (Ibrahim, Sauer, and Yassine 1976, 44). Surveyors also speak with resident populations to learn anything they can, such as the local names for the site, ownership, its history, and so forth. Pottery sherds and other artifacts are systematically collected from all parts of the various sites; these finds are sealed in plastic bags, labeled, and later "read" for chronological purposes. Written observations are also made for each site; these may include topography, visible structures, water sources, and elevation. Finally, photographs are usually taken of each site.

Sampling: *selection of representative remains from which archaeologists draw general conclusions.*

Archaeological survey is heavily dependent on the technique of sampling, that is, drawing general conclusions from representative remains (Plog 1976; Mueller 1975). Even though this

> **Paleoecology:** *the study of plant and animal life from the past.*

technique has undergone criticism from some quarters (Bar-Yosef and Goren 1980, 1), when done properly it has proven to be a good indicator of what the archaeologist will discover below the surface through excavation.

Newer and more sophisticated technologies show promise of enhancing field surveying. A cesium magnetometer, for example, can be used to locate features like burial caves by virtue of the "magnetic contrast [that] exist[s] between the feature one wishes to detect and its immediate environment" (McGovern 1981, 126).

The discipline of photogrammetry is also employed quite extensively in survey work: aerial photographs provide surveyors and mapmakers with the measurements of ancient sites (Beale 1982).

> **Photogrammetry:** *the science of providing reliable measurements through photography.*

Surveying Goals

On the regional level, the principal aim of a field survey is to determine settlement history and patterns (Shanks 1982, 41). In other words, the basic objective is to find out what sites were occupied during what periods. Surveys can give insight into the population density of a region during any particular period.

A second purpose is to identify settlements that were permanent and consequently have great potential for future excavation (Ibrahim, Sauer, and Yassine 1976, 44; Meyers, Strange, and Groh 1978, 1; Gophna and Ayalon 1980, 147). In regard to the Yoqne'am regional project the chief archaeologist remarked, "It is essential to conduct a thorough survey of the region at the earliest stage of the project in order to choose the sites for study and to decide how much effort to devote to each such site" (Ben-Tor 1980, 33).

Regional surveys provide information about topography, natural resources, and transportation routes (Kautz 1988, 215). Such data help to reconstruct the paleoecology of the region. Once a region has been analyzed vis-à-vis its capability of supporting life, it can be compared to the environment and economy of neighboring regions (Gophna 1977, 136).

The regional survey also attempts to search out new sites missed by earlier investigators (Miller 1979, 43). It then integrates the previously collected information with the materials still being found in the area.

Sometimes the regional survey serves to describe, map, and photograph sites in the process of being destroyed. That is, it is used for salvage purposes. For example, in the late 1970s "the redeployment of the Israel Defense Forces in the Negev . . . made necessary a large-scale archaeological emergency rescue project, whose aim [was] to record and save from oblivion archaeological sites and historical information concerning the Negev" (Cohen 1979, 250). Surveys in the Negev between December 1978 and July 1979 discovered and recorded approximately thirteen hundred hitherto unknown sites.

> **Salvage archaeology:** *excavation of sites being destroyed either by vandalism or for the sake of new construction.*

The primary objective of surveys of a single tell is to determine the periods during which the city was occupied (Campbell 1968, 19). Such a survey can indicate whether the site was occupied during the Canaanite periods, the Israelite periods, the Roman period, or any other period in ancient (and modern) history. In addition, it can provide evidence of architectural features, natural resources, and even the function of the site.

The Limitations of Surveying

Although surveying is a standard component of archaeological investigation, and few archaeologists would dare not do it, it is not without its critics. The main problem raised is that "surface survey cannot pretend to absolute precision . . . absence of pottery of a particular period does not prove that the site was unoccupied during that period, while presence of rare sherds of a particular period may mean only that a shepherd broke a water jar" (Campbell 1968, 21). In addition, surveys cannot take into account geomorphological changes that destroy or bury sites. Erosion, moving sands, and other natural elements hide sites from archaeological surveying. Therefore, survey work and its results must be used with great caution.

Conclusions drawn from surveys are subject to correction by further surveying and excavation. Surveying is not the final word in archaeology. The work of Nelson Glueck serves as a good example (Levy 1995, 47). In the 1930s Glueck produced a monumental survey of eastern Palestine. On the basis of his discoveries he theorized that there existed a system of Edomite border fortresses during the early Iron Age (thirteenth-twelfth centuries B.C.). Glueck's view was widely accepted. More-recent survey work, however, has demonstrated that Glueck was inaccurate in his ceramic chronology of Edom (MacDonald 1984, 116). In reality, the sites appear to date no earlier than the ninth and eighth centuries B.C. Even the nature of the sites, whether they do in fact constitute a defensive system, has been called into question. Only excavation can answer that question.

An Example

Reports of surveys abound in archaeological literature. (See, e.g., Beit-Arieh 1979; Cohen 1979; Gophna and Ayalon 1980; Meyers, Strange, and Groh 1978). They cover the range from large regions (Miller 1979) to individual finds like a Roman road (Waterhouse and Ibach 1975). Some of the surveys are quite intensive (Ibach 1978) and others are less so.[2] Obviously, the results obtained by these surveys vary in value. We will consider what one such survey can tell us and what it cannot.

A number of surveys have been conducted in the Shephelah region of Israel (Kochavi 1972; Saarisalo 1931). The Shephelah is a low hilly region that lies between the southern coastal plain and the southern Judean mountains. The surface surveys indicate that the pattern of settlement in the area became much denser during Iron Age I than in Late Bronze Age II. As a matter of fact, the number of sites in Iron Age I is almost 50 percent greater. Moreover, whereas sites in the Late

Bronze Age were located on the banks of rivers, settlement during the Iron Age penetrated into all parts of the region.

On the basis of these survey data it appears that there was an influx of new immigrants into the entire Shephelah region. There is little doubt about that conclusion. What the survey cannot tell us is where the immigrants came from. It is not clear whether the settlers came from outside the Shephelah or from the existing cities within the Shephelah. The only way to arrive at a proper answer is to excavate, and even then the matter may be open to debate.

Archaeology in Palestine began "with field surveys carried out from the backs of horses, camels and donkeys, hoping to locate royal cities and other sites mentioned in the Hebrew Bible" (Levy 1995, 45). That is how Edward Robinson, the first American archaeologist in Palestine, conducted his research in the 1830s. He was followed by the likes of Conder and Kitchener's geographical survey of western Palestine in the 1870s. They recorded more than ten thousand sites. Their survey, published in four volumes, included a map covering approximately six thousand square miles. Nelson Glueck, between 1932 and 1947, made extensive surveys of eastern Palestine (Transjordan). He then did a series of surveys in the Negev between 1952 and 1964. Surveys continue to be a mainstay of archaeological work in the Middle East. In fact, the Archaeological Survey of Israel plans to survey all the land of Palestine. A number of volumes of that survey have already appeared in print (Kochavi 1972; Ronen and Olami 1978).

Surface surveys are helpful and necessary archaeological work. They can provide good previews of excavation. And they help to reconstruct the paleoecology of a site or region. The limitations of surveys, however, must be duly recognized. They are merely preliminary work, and any conclusions drawn from them must be considered provisional until the more definitive work of excavation can be undertaken.

Bibliography

Alon, D., and T. Levy. 1980. "Preliminary Note on the Distribution of Chalcolithic Sites on the Wadi Beer-sheba–Lower Wadi Besor Drainage System." *IEJ* 30:140–47.

Bar-Yosef, O., and N. Goren. 1980. "Afterthoughts following Prehistoric Surveys in the Levant." *IEJ* 30:1–16.

Beale, T. W. 1982. "ASOR to Introduce New Photogrammetic Recording and Mapping System for Field Archaeologists and Epigraphists." *ASOR Newsletter* 7:1–3.

Beit-Arieh, I. 1979. "Sinai Survey, 1978–1979." *IEJ* 29:256–57.

Ben-Tor, A. 1980. "The Regional Study." *BAR* 6.2:30–44.

Campbell, E. F. 1968. "The Shechem Area Survey." *BASOR* 190:19–41.

Cohen, R. 1979. "The Negev Archaeological Emergency Project." *IEJ* 29:250–51.

Currid, J. 1984. "The Deforestation of the Foothills of Palestine." *PEQ* 116:1–11.

Gophna, R. 1977. "Archaeological Survey of the Central Coastal Plain, 1977." *TA* 5:136–47.

Gophna, R., and E. Ayalon. 1980. "Survey of the Central Coastal Plain, 1978–1979: Settlement Pattern of the Middle Bronze Age IIA." *TA* 7:147–50.

Ibach, R. 1976. "Archaeological Survey of the Hesban Region." *AUSS* 14:119–26.

———. 1978. "An Intensive Surface Survey at Jalul." *AUSS* 16:215–22.

Ibrahim, M., J. Sauer, and K. Yassine. 1976. "The East Jordan Valley Survey, 1975." *BASOR* 222:41–66.

Kautz, J. R. 1981. "Tracking the Ancient Moabites." *BA* 44.1:27–35.

———. 1988. "Archaeological Surveys." In *Benchmarks in Time and Culture*, ed. J. F. Drinkard, G. L. Mattingly, and J. M. Miller, 209–22. Atlanta: Scholars.

Kochavi, M. 1972. *Judaea, Samaria and the Golan*. Jerusalem: Archaeological Survey of Israel.

Levy, T. 1995. "From Camels to Computers: A Short History of Archaeological Method." *BAR* 21.4:44–51, 64–65.

MacDonald, B. 1984. "The Wadi el-Hasa Archaeological Survey." In *The Answers Lie Below*, ed. H. O. Thompson, 113–28. Lanham, Md.: University Press of America.

McGovern, P. 1981. "Baqʿah Valley Project 1980." *BA* 44.2:126–28.

Meyers, E., J. Strange, and D. Groh. 1978. "The Meiron Excavation Project: Archaeological Survey in Galilee and Golan, 1976." *BASOR* 230:1–24.

Miller, J. M. 1979. "Archaeological Survey of Central Moab: 1978." *BASOR* 234:43–52.

Mueller, J. W., ed. 1975. *Sampling in Archaeology*. Tucson: University of Arizona Press.

Plog, S. 1976. "Relative Efficiencies of Sampling Techniques for Archaeological Surveys." In *The Early Mesoamerican Village*, ed. K. Flannery, 136–58. New York: Academic.

Redman, C. L., and P. J. Watson. 1970. "Systematic Intensive Surface Collection." *AA* 35:279–91.

Ronen, A., and Y. Olami. 1978. *ʿAtlit Map*. Jerusalem: Archaeological Survey of Israel.

Ruppe, R. J. 1966. "The Archaeological Survey: A Defense." *AA* 31:181–88.

Saarisalo, A. 1931. "Topographical Researches in the Shephelah." *JPOS* 11:19.

Schiffer, M., A. Sullivan, and T. Klinger. 1978. "The Design of Archaeological Surveys." *WA* 10:1–28.

Shanks, H. 1982. "On the Surface." *BAR* 8.2:41–43.

Waterhouse, S., and R. Ibach. 1975. "The Topographical Survey." *AUSS* 13:217–33.

Why Dig There? 5
The Ins and Outs
of Site Identification

The next step for the archaeologist is to identify the site about to be excavated. One would think that such a task would be easy, but that is not always the case. It can be a very complex and often arduous pursuit. Therefore, much has been written regarding the methodology of identifying sites and remains (Ben-Arieh 1972; Kallai 1986; Miller 1983).

The most basic problem is that in a great many cases several names are possibilities for a particular site. On the other hand, there may be several candidates for a name that has been historically recorded. For example, the biblical city of Ziklag has been placed at various locations, such as Khirbet Zuheiliqah, Tell Halif, and Tell Sera' (Seger 1984, 47). No consensus has been reached by researchers. On the other side of the issue, there are tells that could be the remains of any number of historical sites. Tell Halif, in the northern Negev, has been variously identified as the biblical cities of Kiriath-sepher, Sharuhen, Ziklag, Hormah, and Rimmon (Borowski 1988, 21). Little agreement exists regarding its identification.

One may ask at this point, why is it so important that a site be identified? Oded Borowski (1988, 22) gets at the heart of the matter when he says, "Identifying an archaeological site with one recorded in a historical text makes it possible to gain a more precise understanding of, among other things, political boundaries, cultural spheres of influence, trade and military movements. Site identification is thus crucial to the reconstruction of the biblical world." For example, the identification and subsequent excavation of Masada allowed modern scholars to gain a greater depth of understanding of Josephus's historical accounts of events there. Identifying sites helps to give meat to the bones, detail to the general picture of history.

So how does one go about site identification? How does an archaeologist give a historically recorded name to a mound of ruins? Or, on the other hand, how does an archaeologist match a mound of ruins with a historically recorded name? Of course, one must begin with a name that has been recorded in a historical document. It could be a name found in the Bible, or in Egyptian texts, or in Josephus, or in any number of ancient writings. For example, Beth Shean appears to have been an important site in antiquity for it is mentioned in the Bible (Josh. 17:11; Judg. 1:27; 1 Sam. 31:12), in the Egyptian Execration Texts (nineteenth century B.C.), in the topographical lists of Thutmosis III and Shishak at Karnak, in the Amarna Letters, and elsewhere. References to the site in the Hellenistic and Roman periods are too many to mention. Because of these frequent citations, the location of the site is of critical importance. We have a variety of resources that can help us identify it.

Modern Nomenclature

A primary source of evidence for site identification is the preservation of numerous ancient names in modern Arabic nomenclature. "The corpus of geographical names in any region comprises a rich source of linguistic, ethnic, historical, and folkloristic information" (Rainey 1978, 1). Accordingly, modern Arabic place-names were one of the main tools employed by the earliest historical geographers in Palestine to identify ancient sites (Miller 1987, 34).

Edward Robinson describes how Eli Smith's fluency in Arabic helped in site identification: "As a preparation for our further journies in Palestine, my companion had taken great pains to collect from various quarters the native names of all those places in those parts which we hoped to visit . . . there was frequent opportunity of making the acquaintance of intelligent Sheikhs and other persons from the towns and villages in that and other districts; and they were in general ready to communicate all they knew respecting the places in their own neighborhood" (1868, 435). Robinson and Smith were able to match dozens of sites with ancient names recorded in the Bible, Josephus, and other sources. Much of their work has stood the test of time.

One of the great surprises of historical geography is the consistency with which ancient names have been preserved in the modern Arabic toponymy of Palestine. Yohanan Aharoni comments on this phenomenon: "Towns were usually built on fixed locations throughout the course of long periods, and their names have been preserved with amazing consistency . . . a new settlement was nearly always founded on the same ancient hill, the old name being preserved in spite of all the changes in the population's composition" (1967, 94–95). The name continued even when the sociological or cultural group occupying the site was displaced by another. For example, when Israel drove out the Canaanites and settled at the old sites, they adopted many of the Canaanite names (such as Megiddo and Hazor) (Richardson 1969, 104).

New names generally proved unsuccessful in replacing the old. There were a few exceptions, however. For instance, in Judges 18 the biblical writer tells of the destruction of the Canaanite city of Laish by the Danites: they

> **Toponymy:** *the systematic study of place names within a geographic region.*

"came to Laish, to a people quiet and secure, and struck them with the edge of the sword; and they burned the city with fire. . . . And they rebuilt the city and lived in it. And they called the name of the city Dan, after the name of Dan their father who was born in Israel; however, the name of the city formerly was Laish" (vv. 27–29). Similarly, in Numbers 32:37–38 the names of certain cities east of the Jordan, such as Baal-meon, were altered. Such examples, however, are few and far between.

The transmission of ancient names to modern Arabic was often a complex process (Brinner 1995). The complexities in the process were recognized early in the investigation of ancient Palestine. Edward Palmer, who did a great deal of work on the Arabic name lists compiled by Conder and Kitchener, commented:

> To determine the exact meaning of Arabic topographical names is by no means easy. Some are descriptive of physical features, but even these are

often obsolete or distorted words. Others are derived from long since for-
gotten incidents, or owners whose memory has passed away. Others again
are survivals of older Nabataean, Hebrew, Canaanite, and other names,
either quite meaningless in Arabic, or having an Arabic form in which the
original sound is perhaps more or less preserved, but the sense entirely lost.
Occasionally Hebrew, especially biblical and talmudic names, remain
scarcely altered. [1881, iii–iv]

Sometimes a name was detached from its original site and attached
to another in the same vicinity. That is what happened to Beth
Shean. Conder and Kitchener found the Arab village of Beisan on
a ridge near the original tell (Rainey 1982, 219). Place names could
also be transferred to the shrine of a local sheikh, or to a nearby water
source, or to more-modern remains in an area (Rainey 1976, 826).

Linguistic alterations often occurred between an ancient name
and a modern one. Thus the village near the ancient mound of Beth
Shean was called Beisan. Another type of problem in the transmission of names is suggested in the case of the biblical city of Ophrah.
Historical citations led Edward Robinson to locate Ophrah at the
mound of et-Taiyibeh. The match was not based on any similarity
or relationship between the two names. Many decades later, R. Hartmann (1911) proposed that the principle of euphemism was at work
in the situation. The name Ophrah sounds quite like the Arabic *ifrit*,
which means "demon." So the Arab inhabitants consciously changed
the name to its opposite, et-Taiyibeh, "the favored one."

Even with these entanglements, the rate of the survival of ancient
names into the modern period is astounding. An additional obstacle
was that during the Roman-Byzantine times Semitic names were often
replaced by Greek or Latin titles. Beth Shean, for instance, was called
Scythopolis. But the ancient name survived despite the interruption.
Likewise the Old Testament city of Lod was called Diospolis during
the Roman period, but the name Lod (Ludd) resurfaced after the Arab
conquest and repopulation of the site (Rainey 1976, 826).

Texts

Another approach to site identification is through textual materials
(Wainwright 1962). Today we possess many collateral written sources
that can provide historical, geographical, and topological clues.

Ancient written sources. Contemporary sources, of course, play a crucial role in site identification. The Bible was the primary textual resource for early travelers, such as Edward Robinson and Eli Smith. Though not without its problems as a geographical guide, the Bible remains a most valuable tool (Miller 1983). The early researches also made use of rabbinic literature, in particular, the Talmud (Neubauer 1868). Those writings are helpful because "the biblical toponyms are often discussed in relation to their Second-Temple counterparts" (Rainey 1978, 12). Also available to the nineteenth-century investigators were early translations of the Bible, like the Septuagint, which reflect an early exegesis of topography.

In our day and age, much more textual evidence is available to the historical geographer. Ancient writings like the Ugaritic texts (Richardson 1969, 97), the Dead Sea Scrolls, the Arad Letters, the Lachish Letters, the Ebla tablets, and numerous Egyptian inscriptions provide a massive topographical database for ancient Palestine. Cities like Beth Shean, Megiddo, and Hazor are mentioned often in Egyptian military and travel itineraries. A close inspection of those documents can help to determine locations.

Writings of early Christianity. The early church fathers are also important witnesses to the location of ancient sites. At the top of the list is the *Onomasticon* written by Eusebius of Caesarea. "Eusebius' interest in the Old and New Testaments and in the identification of the sites mentioned in them led him to the composition of this work, which was enhanced by his Palestinian roots and consequent familiarity with local topography. For each book of the Bible, Eusebius lists, alphabetically, the names of the towns, mountains, rivers, districts, plains, and deserts that are mentioned. . . . He often relates the ancient site to a contemporary one" (Borowski 1988, 22). Though not always accurate, Eusebius's gazetteer is important for researchers today because it is seventeen hundred years closer to antiquity than we are. Also worth consulting are Arab geographers from the medieval period.

> **Gazetteer:** *an index of geographical names.*

The survey of western Palestine. The expedition led by Lieutenants Conder and Kitchener from 1871 to 1877 continues to make a major contribution to the geographical knowledge of Palestine, both ancient and modern. In fact, most maps used today are based upon their original survey. Their reports included both a huge map of Palestine divided into twenty-six sections and ten thousand sites listed alphabetically in the text according to their Arabic names and then transliterated into English. Also to be consulted when one is trying to identify a site are many of the early travelers in Palestine—people like Robinson, Tobler, Guérin—who recorded names and described sites before the "onset of modern political and population changes" (Borowski 1988, 23).

Archaeology

A final resource for site identification has been available for only the last century or so: archaeological investigation. Excavation can uncover inscriptional evidence corroborating a site's name (de Vries 1994, 217). For example, excavations on the mound of Beth Shean unearthed a stele from the time of Seti I that included the name of the ancient town. Similarly, confirming that Tell el-Mutesillim is the site of the Megiddo mentioned on a relief at Karnak celebrating the exploits of the pharaoh Shishak is the discovery of a piece of a Shishak stele on the mound itself.

Some scholars argue that a close correlation between the stratigraphy of a mound and the known history of a particular town is confirming evidence of identification (Miller 1987, 35–36). This is dangerous, however. The correlation may be accidental. Thus this type of evidence cannot stand alone: "Even the presence of stratified remains corresponding to the historical periods of a town is not valid evidence for identification unless the locale and other factors harmonize with the texts" (Rainey 1976, 827). On the other hand, a lack of correspondence between the stratigraphy of a mound and the known history of a particular town does not necessarily mean that the mound is not the site. Archaeology is by nature selective; it can provide a mere sampling of the remains of a site. While the lack of remains from a period is suggestive, it is not conclusive.

An Example: Ziklag

We have seen that site identification is a complex process. Normally it requires several resources being used together to make a positive match. Rarely does one resource alone secure an identification. Thus, when an archaeologist wants to determine the name of a site, all of the many aspects of historical geography must be taken into account. Even then there is no guarantee of success. More often than not, uncertainty remains even after all the research and study.

As an example of the doubt that pervades the process of site identification, let us consider the city of Ziklag. After the conquest of Canaan it became part of the tribal allotment of Simeon (Josh. 19:5), although it was quite near the area of the tribe of Judah (Josh. 15:21, 31). It appears to have later fallen into the hands of the Philistines; Achish of Gath, however, deeded the site to David (1 Sam. 27:5–6). Ziklag was soon thereafter destroyed by marauding Amalekites who carried off its women and children (1 Sam. 30). David pursued and made war on the Amalekites. The site, then, was a fairly important one in biblical history.

The question is, where is Ziklag? What mound is the name Ziklag to be associated with? Joe D. Seger comments: "The problem of identifying the actual geographical site of the biblical city of Ziklag has exercised students of the Bible and archaeology since early in the century; however, despite the fact that biblical accounts provide a number of clues, and after almost a full century of intensive archaeological exploration and study, no firm consensus has yet emerged" (1984, 47). Seger himself concludes that it should be located at the mound of Tell Halif. Others disagree: Aharoni places Ziklag at Tell Sera', and William F. Albright proposes the site of Khirbet Zuheiliqah (Aharoni 1967, 25).

Let us turn to the three major resources for site identification to see if we can locate Ziklag. First of all, there is no similarity between the name Ziklag and any known place-names in the general area where the site is thought to be. The name Ziklag is simply not preserved in any modern Arabic nomenclature. Thus our first possible resource proves to be a dead end.

Second, the historical records of the Bible do provide a general location. Ziklag is mentioned fifteen times in the Bible. The first reference to the site lists it as one of "the cities at the extremity of the tribe of the sons of Judah toward the border of Edom in the south [Negev]" (Josh. 15:21, 31). Ziklag was also deemed to be part of the tribal allotment to Simeon (Josh. 19:5), which was in the northern part of the Negev. That Ziklag is in the Negev is confirmed by other passages (1 Sam. 30:1, 14). When David pursued the Amalekites who had destroyed Ziklag, two hundred of his men "were too exhausted to cross the brook Besor" (v. 10), which in modern Arabic is called the Wadi esh-Shari'ah (Borowski 1988, 24). Ziklag must be located north of this stream because the Amalekites dwelt in the central and southern areas of the Negev (Exod. 17) and were returning there. In addition, Ziklag was situated in an area disputed by Israel and Philistia (1 Sam. 27:5–7). That would appear to place Ziklag in the southern part of the Shephelah (foothill region) that borders on the northern Negev.

The number of mounds in that area is limited. In fact, the two most likely candidates are Tell Halif and Tell Sera'. But even that conclusion is somewhat dubious. There are other possibilities; for example, Tell Haror, Khirbet Zuheiliqah, and even Tell Beit Mirsim. Thus we are left with a general idea but nothing conclusive concerning the location of Ziklag.

Our third resource is to analyze the remains found in excavations of the likely candidates. We know from the Bible that the site of Ziklag will produce specific evidence: (1) remains from the period of the judges, early-middle Iron Age I; (2) remains from late Iron Age I, the era of David (the tenth century B.C.); (3) a destruction level from the tenth century B.C. (the Amalekite incursion); (4) remains from Iron Age II (1 Sam. 27:6); and (5) remains from the Persian period (Neh. 11:28).

Seger has demonstrated that the excavations at Tell Halif have uncovered materials meeting all five historical criteria (1984, 48–52). The greatest weakness in identifying Ziklag with Tell Halif is the minimal amount of Iron Age I remains at the mound. A mere handful of materials have been discovered from that time. This is curious given that the most significant biblical records of Ziklag cover that period.

Eliezer Oren (1982), on the other hand, has concluded that the site of Tell Sera' fits the historical picture better. Significant remains have been uncovered from all of the historical periods during which we know there was activity at Ziklag. The only major problem, and an enormous one it is, is that there is no evidence of destruction of the site in the tenth century B.C. Oren reports what appears to have been a peaceful transition from Iron Age I to Iron Age II (p. 163).

So where is Ziklag? In an important work Borowski (1988) argues convincingly that the biblical site of Rimmon (Judah) ought to be located at Tell Halif. If he is correct, then a prime candidate for Ziklag has been removed from consideration. Is Ziklag, then, at Tell Sera'? Possibly. It is the best candidate. To say more than that would be to go beyond the evidence at hand. Our efforts to locate Ziklag have clearly shown that site identification is anything but a simple task.

Bibliography

Aharoni, Y. 1967. *The Land of the Bible*. Philadelphia: Westminster.

Ben-Arieh, Y. 1972. "The Geographical Exploration of the Holy Land." *PEQ* 104:81–92.

Borowski, O. 1988. "The Biblical Identity of Tel Halif." *BA* 51.1:21–27.

Brinner, W. M. 1995. "Some Problems in the Arabic Transmission of Biblical Names." In Z. Zevit et al., *Solving Riddles and Untying Knots*, 19–27. Winona Lake, Ind.: Eisenbrauns.

de Vries, B. 1994. "What's in a Name: The Anonymity of Ancient Umm el-Jimal." *BA* 57.4:215–19.

Hartmann, R. 1911. "Zum Ortsnamen aṭ-Ṭajjiba." *Zeitschrift der deutschen morgenländischen Gesellschaft* 65:536–38.

Kallai, Z. 1986. *Historical Geography of the Bible*. Jerusalem: Magnes.

Miller, J. M. 1983. "Site Identification: A Problem Area in Contemporary Biblical Scholarship." *ZDPV* 99:119–29.

———. 1987. "Biblical Maps: How Reliable Are They?" *BR* 3.4:32–41.

Neubauer, A. 1868. *La Géographie du Talmud*. Paris: Michel Levy frères.

Oren, E. D. 1982. "Ziklag—A Biblical City on the Edge of the Negev." *BA* 45.3:155–66.

Palmer, E. H. 1881. *The Survey of Western Palestine: Arabic and English Name Lists Collected during the Survey by Lieutenants Conder and Kitchener*. London: Palestine Exploration Fund.

Rainey, A. 1976. "Sites, Ancient, Identification of." In *Interpreter's Dictionary of the Bible, Supplementary Volume*, ed. K. Crim, 825–27. Nashville: Abingdon.

———. 1978. "The Toponymics of Eretz-Israel." *BASOR* 231:1–17.

———. 1982. "Historical Geography—The Link between Historical and Archeological Interpretation." *BA* 45.4:217–23.

Richardson, M. E. J. 1969. "Hebrew Toponyms." *TB* 20:95–104.

Robinson, E. 1868. *Biblical Researches in Palestine I*. Boston: Crocker and Brewster.

Seger, J. 1984. "The Location of Biblical Ziklag." *BA* 47.1:47–53.

Wainwright, F. T. 1962. *Archaeology and Place Names and History*. London: Routledge and Paul.

In the Beginning: How To Excavate a Tell

6

At this point the archaeologist has completed much of the preparatory work for excavation. He has studied the historical records pertaining to the site, he has done his work of identification, and he has completed an archaeological survey of the site itself. Now the excavator stands atop the tell ready to excavate thousands of years of history in the form of a three-dimensional jigsaw puzzle (Lance 1981, 22). What is the digger's goal? It is to learn about the people who occupied the tell, their history and culture, stratum by stratum. In order to accomplish that goal, the archaeologist must unravel the mound piece by piece. This process is actually a backward methodology—the last materials to be deposited are the first to be excavated.

Systems of excavation are almost as numerous as the number of excavators. And there is no agreement as to the proper manner of digging. Mortimer Wheeler put it this way: "There is no right way of digging but there are many wrong ones." The intention in this chapter is not to debate the various systems of excavation, but to concentrate on the primary concepts involved. In other words, this is not the place to get bogged down in details or minor differences. We will simply consider the basic techniques of archaeological excavation.

History of Excavation Methods

The development of archaeological methodology can be divided into three periods (Toombs 1982, 90). The early phase, before World War I, was characterized by inadequate control of excavation procedures. Large areas were opened without proper oversight. Supervisory staffs were insufficient; often only one or two people directed the work. Record keeping was deficient; in those early days the principal archaeologist kept the only excavation diary. Frequently, only the most significant artifacts and architectural features were recorded. Almost everything else was lost to history. In addition, there was little interest in the earth or soil layers in which remains were found. Soil was thought to be merely an obstruction to be dumped off the site.

Making matters worse was the fact that before "World War II, most archaeologists excavated in arbitrary levels, for example, stripping off 30-cm.-thick layers of debris across the area with large picks and hoes" (Van Beek 1988, 135–36). The depth of the excavation was often random; and, therefore, intrusion of material from one layer into another was commonplace. The early excavators simply ignored the natural deposition of earth layers. Consequently, excavation reports from this early phase are of minimal value: their assigning of remains to levels and dates is untrustworthy.

Between the world wars, strides were made in archaeological methodology. The most important development was the establishment of a general chronological framework for the history and archaeology of Palestine. Based upon ceramic typology, this framework was delineated by William F. Albright at Tell Beit Mirsim and by the University of Chicago excavations at Megiddo.

The principal method of excavation at this time was the architectural approach. Its aim was wide-scale exposure of architectural units. Careful stratigraphic analysis was not considered all that worthwhile; indeed, strata were analyzed mainly on the basis "of the relation between different architectural components such as walls and floor levels" (Mazar 1990, 21). Clusters of pottery found on the floor of a building were especially important because they reflected the latest phase of its occupation. Sometimes the architectural method is called the Reisner-Fisher technique after G. A. Reisner and C. S. Fisher, who applied it to their excavations at Megiddo in the 1920s and 1930s.

> **Reisner-Fisher method:** *an archaeological approach that stresses broad exposure of architecture.*

After the Second World War two opposing methodologies dominated the archaeology of Palestine. The first was the traditional architectural method. The second approach was the Wheeler-Kenyon method, named after the two influential archaeologists who promoted the system.

Mortimer Wheeler was a British archaeologist (1890–1976) who spent his life digging large sites in Britain with great precision. His best excavation was the campaign at Maiden Castle, Dorset, a major fort whose complex history he was able to unravel (Fagan 1996). He was especially well known for training a generation of archaeologists in his excavation techniques, which he set forth in his classic study *Archaeology from the Earth* (1954).

> **Wheeler-Kenyon method:** *an archaeological approach that stresses identification of the strata in the soil.*

Wheeler believed the key to archaeology was accurate excavation, observation, and recording of occupation levels. His basic thesis was that "the observation of superimposed layers and the features and artifacts in them would give one an accurate chronology to work with, an essential framework for studying the numerous pot fragments and other finds from the dig" (Fagan 1978, 17). Rather than adopting the architectural approach, which relied on the records of surveyors and architects, Wheeler was convinced that greater attention needed to be paid to the interrelation of structures, objects, and debris. Identification of the strata in the soil was paramount in his system.

The British archaeologist Kathleen Kenyon agreed wholeheartedly with Wheeler: "The science of excavation is dependent on the interpretation of the stratification of a site, that is to say, the layers of soil associated with it" (Kenyon 1957, 69). Her excavations at Jericho in the 1950s applied to the archaeology of Palestine Wheeler's focus on the layers of debris.

The system requires, first of all, a careful digging of test trenches in order to determine the precise stratification of the tell prior to full-scale excavation (Albright 1971, 21). That provides a preview of the soil layers that will be encountered later. Unlike the architectural method, the subsequent excavation digs up small squares instead of clearing whole areas (Moorey 1991, 95). Standing sections called balks are left from the surface on down. The balk records the vertical relationship of one soil layer to another and the relationship of the architecture to these various layers. The system thus provides detailed control of the excavation area.

Balks: *unexcavated sections left standing between the squares of an archaeological dig to record the relationship of soil layers.*

The greatest weakness of the Wheeler-Kenyon method is "the lack of comprehensive horizontal exposure" (Mazar 1990, 25). The excavated squares are often too narrow. A broader exposure is needed, such as that afforded by the architectural method. A second problem with the Wheeler-Kenyon method is an inadequate awareness of "site formation processes," that is, the cultural and natural activities that formed the deposits of the tell (Dever 1992, 363). The system is precise in regard to soil layers and their relationships to architecture and other objects, but it tells us little about the history of technology, trade, and so forth.

Both of these problems have been addressed in recent years. The lack of broad exposure has been answered by the integration of the two basic systems: the architectural method and the stratigraphical method are now employed together. A balance is achieved in that digs now uncover large areas but with proper stratigraphic control and analysis of soil layers (Dever 1974).

The second problem is being solved with the application of the so-called New Archaeology to the study of Palestine. This multidisciplinary approach includes both social and natural sciences.

New Archaeology: *a recent movement that calls for an interdisciplinary approach in archaeology.*

Excavators "began to pay attention to floral and faunal remains, traces of past subsistence systems, evidence for environmental change, and indeed *all* data on material culture that by chance had been preserved in the archaeological record" (Dever 1992, 355). Accordingly, studies like ecology, ethnology, and general systems theory have become part and parcel of excavation work in Palestine (Dever 1981, 15).

Excavation Today

Much has been written regarding excavation theory and procedure (Blakely and Toombs 1981; Chapman 1986; Dever and Lance

1978; Franken and Franken-Battershill 1963, 8–18). It is our purpose here to provide a brief look at the basic steps in most excavation projects in Palestine: excavation, proper recording, and publishing.

Excavation

The excavation normally begins by drawing a grid system on a topographical map of the tell itself (Fritz 1994, 56). The purpose of this plotting is to precisely locate the areas selected for excavation and to leave other specific areas unexcavated, so that future archaeologists may do further work at the site.

After the excavation areas have been chosen, individual squares (usually 5 by 5 meters) are marked off by metal posts. This grid of squares is "the framework for the excavation; balks left between the squares form sections of the earth layers, and examination of these levels during excavation enables more precise stratigraphic observation" (Mazar 1990, 24).

Prior to full-scale work, the archaeologist will often sink a test trench or probe to get a preview of what lies below. Such a pit can be useful in anticipating the stratigraphy and chronology of the area to be excavated.

Once the digging begins, the primary focus of the excavation is control in both the vertical and horizontal dimensions. Such control "is exercised by the combination of technique and supervision" (Toombs 1982, 89). Today, supervisory staffs are large, with each square under the direction of a staff member. Every square supervisor keeps a daily journal of the excavation work, finds, and observations.

Digging is done by hand. Depending on the situation, different types of tools are employed. For example, for the removal of loose, sterile debris a pick and a hoe can be used. For more delicate operations, such as the recovery of a burial, a dental pick and a small brush are better suited.

In the process of digging, the soil of a layer is removed, placed in a bucket, emptied in a wheelbarrow, and deposited in a predesignated dump area. Pottery sherds are separated from the soil layer and collected in numbered baskets or buckets. The pottery is later "read" so that a general date may be assigned to its soil layer.

The appearance of a new layer must be noted; this is accomplished by recognizing changes in the color and composition of the earth. *The Munsell Soil Color Charts* are very helpful in this process

(Munsell 1954). New baskets are provided for each layer, so that the pottery from each layer may be kept separate.

If walls of a structure or installation begin to emerge, they are excavated carefully and assigned locus numbers. As walls are being revealed, the archaeologist keeps an eye open for a floor. It should be noted that the "presence of a floor is often heralded by an increase in the number and size of pottery sherds" (Fritz 1994, 57). Sherds found on the floor of a building usually reflect the latest date of its occupation.

The sections (or balks) of a square require special attention. Revealing what layers have been dug through, they need to be kept straight and neat. They function as a necessary control vis-à-vis stratigraphic sequence.

Recording

Excavation is destruction. Once remains have been removed, they cannot be replaced. Therefore it is essential that an archaeological project employ a detailed and comprehensive system of recording. A typical system consists of four basic parts:

1. *The notes and drawings of square supervisors.* Observations of an excavation square must be chronicled daily by a staff supervisor. The excavation log includes a list of finds (basket/bucket list), a locus list with a summary or description of each locus, a top plan, and section drawings.

Figure 4 is an example of a top plan. On the plan are indicated the field and area of excavation, the date of the drawing, the scale, and direction. In the depiction of the excavation square

Section: *a vertical balk face that shows the soil layers.*

the various locus numbers designating specific layers, walls, and installations are recorded and inserted in a rectangle (e.g., 026). Also recorded at the end of each day are elevations in relation to sea level (e.g., x 63.54 meters). The precise locations where pottery and other finds were discovered may also be indicated on the top plan.

The square supervisor also provides section drawings. Included in these depictions of the vertical sections of the balks are the locus numbers of the various layers, walls, and floors (see fig. 5).

Figure 4
Top Plan of an Excavation Area

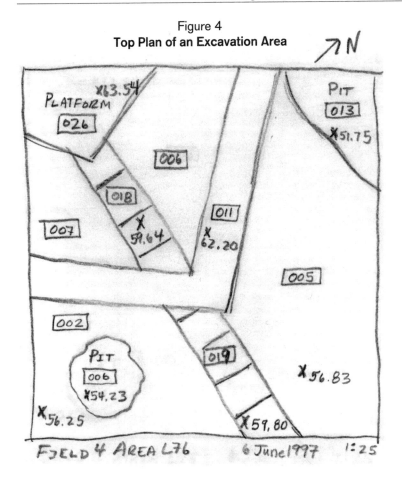

2. *Architectural drawings.* The job of the project architect is to draw all structures and installations unearthed during excavation. Every stone is measured and drawn to scale. After digging

> **In situ:** *the original setting of an object found in an excavation.*

is completed, the architect draws a set of plans reflecting the individual strata. An idea of what the buildings of a city were like during particular periods then begins to emerge. Whereas the plans of the archaeological supervisors focus on a square, the architectural drawings are inclusive of the entire excavation area.

Figure 5
Vertical Section of an Excavation Area

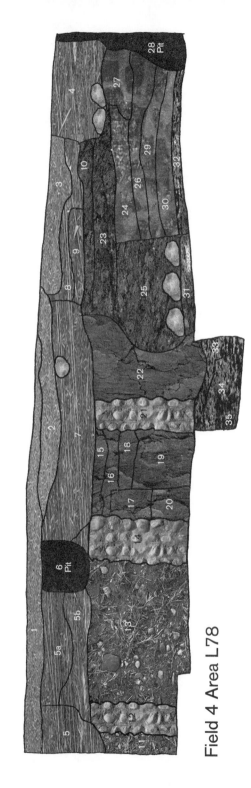

Field 4 Area L78

3. *Photography*. Everything that is discovered in an excavation, save debris and sherds from the main body of a vessel (which offer little information about the original), ought to be photographed. This ought to be done when the object is in situ. Photography provides visual documentation of where something was found and how it relates to other materials in the tell. This recordkeeping must be done well, because it is the basis of what will later be published.

4. *Index of finds* (Moorey 1981, 63). For each object uncovered, except for pottery, an index card is assigned. On the card is significant information such as the locus in which the piece was discovered, the date, and a general description of the object (see fig. 6). These objects are later cleaned, drawn, and photographed. Some finds may also need restoration and conservation work.

Figure 6
Index Card Reporting the Discovery of a Small Find

AREA L SUPERVISOR	JC

| SQUARE 78 | LOCUS | 027 |
| OBJECT 07 | DATE | 17/6 |

DESCRIPTION: FISHERMAN'S NEEDLE,
  IRON, 3" LONG

With the completion of excavation and recording, the excavator should have good and proper data to begin to reconstruct the history of a tell. "When the season's work is over, the excavator thus has a complete record of the site. He has plans of walls which he can prove are contemporary by their association with the same floors. He has pottery and objects from the various levels, with measured sections to prove to which of the various building periods they belong" (Kenyon 1939, 35).

Publication

The final step is to publish the results of excavation. Indeed, "the only means available for reconstructing the excavation of a tell is the report or publication. Therefore, it behooves all archaeologists to excavate as carefully as possible, to record the excavations completely, and to publish full data and the most reasoned interpretations of those data as their knowledge and imaginations allow" (Van Beek 1988, 133–34). This step requires systematic analysis and interpretation of the remains of a dig. Such analysis and publication are essential, because digging is only a means to an end: the understanding of humanity's complex and changing relationship with the environment (Fagan 1978, 18).

Bibliography

Albright, W. F. 1971. *The Archaeology of Palestine*. Rev. ed. Gloucester, Mass.: Peter Smith.

Blakely, J. A., and L. E. Toombs. 1981. *The Tell el-Hesi Field Manual*. Winona Lake, Ind.: Eisenbrauns.

Chapman, R. 1986. "Excavation Techniques and Recording Systems: A Theoretical Study." *PEQ* 118:5–20.

Dever, W. G. 1974. "Two Approaches to Archaeological Method—The Architectural and the Stratigraphic." *EI* 11:1–8.

———. 1981. "The Impact of the 'New Archaeology' on Syro-Palestinian Archaeology." *BASOR* 242:14–29.

———. 1992. "Archaeology, Syro-Palestinian and Biblical." *ABD* 1:354–67.

Dever, W. G., and H. D. Lance, eds. 1978. *A Manual of Field Excavation*. Cincinnati: Hebrew Union College.

Fagan, B. 1978. *Quest for the Past*. Prospect Heights, Ill.: Waveland.

———. 1996. "Mortimer Wheeler." In *The Oxford Companion to Archaeology*, ed. B. Fagan, 755. New York: Oxford University Press.

Franken, H. J., and C. A. Franken-Battershill. 1963. *A Primer of Old Testament Archaeology*. Leiden: Brill.

Fritz, V. 1994. *An Introduction to Biblical Archaeology*. Sheffield, Eng.: Sheffield Academic Press.

Kenyon, K. 1939. "Excavation Methods in Palestine." *PEQ* 71:29–37.

———. 1957. *Beginning in Archaeology*. New York: Praeger.

Lance, H. D. 1981. *The Old Testament and the Archaeologist*. Philadelphia: Fortress.

Mazar, A. 1990. *Archaeology of the Land of the Bible*. New York: Doubleday.

Moorey, P. R. S. 1981. *Excavation in Palestine*. Guildford, Eng.: Lutterworth.

———. 1991. *A Century of Biblical Archaeology*. Louisville: Westminster John Knox.

Munsell, A. H. 1954. *Munsell Soil Color Charts*. Baltimore: Munsell.

Toombs, L. E. 1982. "The Development of Palestinian Archaeology as a Discipline." BA 45.2:89–91.

Van Beek, G. 1988. "Excavation of Tells." In *Benchmarks in Time and Culture*, ed. J. F. Drinkard, G. L. Mattingly, and J. M. Miller, 131–67. Atlanta: Scholars.

Wheeler, M. 1954. *Archaeology from the Earth*. Oxford: Clarendon.

Petrie, Pottery, and Potsherds

7

The study of pottery is a fundamental aspect of every excavation in Palestine (Lapp 1961, 1). This has been true since William M. Flinders Petrie dug at Tell el-Hesi in 1890. Convinced of the immense value of ceramic study he claimed: "Once settle the pottery of a country, and the key is in our hands for all future explorations. A single glance at a mound of ruins, even without dismounting, will show as much to anyone who knows the styles of pottery, as weeks of work may reveal to a beginner" (Petrie 1891, 40).

Archaeologists who do not pay close attention to the pottery of an excavation undermine the value and significance of any digging that they do. Gottlieb Schumacher's ignorance and avoidance of ceramic work at Megiddo at the turn to the twentieth century made his finds of little service to later archaeologists (Albright 1971, 33). He is by no means the only culprit in this regard.

The Chronological Significance of Pottery

What is it about pottery that makes it so valuable for archaeology? In the first place, pottery is the most basic and useful tool for developing the chronology of a site.[1] As G. Ernest Wright said, "Given a sufficient quantity of broken or whole pieces from a given stratum, the date of that stratum can be established" (Wright 1962, 24; see also Borowski 1982). In addition, the archaeologist can compare pottery gathered from various sites and thus come up with a relative dat-

> Potsherd: *a ceramic fragment; a broken piece of pottery.*

ing sequence for an area and even a chronological order for all of Palestine (Mazar 1990, 28). Simply put, pottery "is incomparably the most useful class of object for dating" (Albright 1957, 49).

The great value of pottery for sequence dating derives from its durability. Although whole vessels are fragile and break easily, potsherds are virtually indestructible. They do not decay, rust, burn, corrode, evaporate, or melt. Pottery is found in every layer of a site because it lasts (Borowski 1988, 223).

> Diagnostic sherd: *a pottery fragment that gives indication of the original vessel's style and date; normally a rim, handle, or base.*

The importance of pottery for chronology also arises from its changeability. That is to say, the features of pottery vessels (such as design and shape) were remarkably standardized during any given period in a region. However, these traits changed at frequent intervals. In other words, each period had its own distinctive and typical pottery. Archaeologists are able to date any level or stratum in a site by the type of pottery that appears in it. Among the elements of pottery that help to distinguish one period from another are form, decoration, ware, and method of manufacture (Crowfoot 1932; Gonen 1973; Honeyman 1939).

> Burnishing: *polishing pottery to seal pores and to create a lustrous finish.*

Form variations. Every potsherd displays characteristics of the original whole vessel. There are two types of potsherds. The first are called indicators or diagnostic sherds. Included in this category are rims, handles, and bases. These are very helpful in identifying the shape and use of a vessel because their appearance changed at frequent intervals. The second category of sherds is the body sherds; these are much less helpful in determining the shape and purpose of a jar.

Variations of the shape of rims, handles, and bases are representative of different periods. Iron Age II, for example, is represented by jugs with a double, deeply grooved rim, a form unknown in the

Late Bronze Age. Some periods are characterized by kraters with multiple handles (from four to eight in Iron Age I); others are not (e.g., Late Bronze Age). The bowls of certain strata have predominantly flat bases, and the bowls of other layers have curved bottoms. Thus ceramic form serves as a key indicator of the sequencing of a site and a region.

> Slip: *a thin surface coat of untempered clay.*

Decoration. Pottery was also decorated in different ways in different periods. A vessel might be shaved, incised, or punctured; it might be surfaced with slip, wash, paint, or glaze; it might be polished or burnished. Some periods used ornamental techniques more than did others, and thus these techniques are good chronological indicators. For instance, little use was made of painted decoration in Israelite pottery, but in Late Bronze Canaanite pottery it was used often. The cooking pots of the early Middle Bronze Age (MB II A) were characterized by perforations and external decoration that looked like a rope. Cooking pots from the following periods (MB II B–C) were adorned differently. Variation in pottery decoration between periods is almost endless.

> Wash: *a thin, watery coating of paint.*

The ceramic of some periods is coated with slip, a thin surface of fine, untempered clay that is applied to the vessel to make it harder and thus easier to paint and to polish. A slip also renders the pot less permeable, and it may also change the color of the vessel. The clay used for slip is finer and thinner than that used in the body of the jar.[2] Other ages preferred to cover pottery with wash, a thin or watery coating of paint spread on the outside of a vessel. Sometimes jars were burnished, that is, rubbed to make them shiny and glossy.

> Ware: *the combination of clay and nonplastics used to make pottery.*

Ware. The essence of pottery is its ware, that is, its particular combination of clay and nonplastics. Sometimes called inclu-

> Temper: *a substance added to clay to harden ware, lessen shrinking, and stop cracking.*

> Grog: *ground-up pots used as temper.*

sions, the nonplastics are the minerals or fossils added to clay to produce pottery. The ware of pottery varies by region because raw materials often differ by region. The ware is also a clue to chronology because certain periods preferred some nonplastics over others.

> Levigation: *mixing clay with water to rid it of impurities.*

Manufacturing. The preparation of clay by a potter also changed throughout the centuries. In Palestine, Neolithic and Chalcolithic ceramic was formed by hand; the slow wheel made its first appearance at Tell el-Farah and Megiddo about 3000 B.C.; and the fast wheel did not arrive on the scene until Middle Bronze II. The manner of firing evolved too, from the simple campfire to the oven and to the more elaborate kiln. Potters used a variety of techniques that often differed from one period to the next. For instance, some craftsmen employed levigation methods to help purify the ware (Lapp 1975, 35). In addition, they added numerous materials to the clay to harden it, minimize shrinking, and prevent cracking. This

> Ostraca: *pottery sherds containing writing.*

process is called tempering. Straw, dung, sand, salt, and grog are a few of the substances employed in antiquity. Specific periods and locations normally adopted one technique over others. For example, dark-faced burnished ware of the Neolithic period almost always contains straw temper, whereas other periods did not use it at all.

The Epigraphic Significance of Pottery

Sometimes excavations uncover sherds with inscriptions written on them. These are called ostraca (ostracon in the singular). The inscriptions are normally written in ink and short, ranging from a few words to several lines. It appears that some of them were written in time of crisis when other writing materials were unavailable.

Perhaps the most well known ostraca found in Palestine are the Lachish Letters, uncovered at the site of Tell ed-Duweir between 1932 and 1938 (Torczyner 1938, 11–18). Twenty-one ostraca were discovered with nearly one hundred complete and fragmentary lines. They all date to the final Judahite occupation at Lachish before its destruction at the hands of Nebuchadnezzar in 586 B.C. and thus have great historical significance (Di Vito 1992). The numerous ostraca from Samaria are also of great interest. The hope for similar discoveries is one reason that in most excavations today all pottery sherds are washed and examined.

The Sociological Significance of Pottery

In the 1930s G. Ernest Wright made a prediction regarding the benefits of ceramic study: "Its greatest value at present is undoubtedly chronological; yet more expert studies in the future will perhaps allow the student of ethnology, commerce, and related subjects, to make far-reaching deductions from ceramic evidence, for which at present there is so little solid ground" (Wright 1937, 1). His prognostication has come to pass. Archaeologists today use ceramic analysis to better understand the cultural context in which vessels were made (Shepard 1956; Nicklin 1971; Johnston 1974 and 1986). Indeed, a "comprehensive approach to the ceramic technology of Palestine may provide a living dimension to the archaeological record" (Glock 1975, 10). This field of research is called ceramic ecology (Matson 1965).

Ceramic ecology can provide us with important insights into various areas of ancient culture:

1. The nature of the ceramic industry at a particular site or in a region. Pottery analysis yields information about the technology of the craftsman, the organization of potters, and the type of workshop. It can, for example, tell us if the potters were using a single wheel, a double wheel, or no wheel at all.
2. The diffusion of a style of pottery throughout a region. Ceramic ecology seeks to explain the mechanism for that diffusion and its implication about trade.
3. The function of pottery in a typical household (Wood 1990).

In short, the sociological study of pottery helps us to reconstruct the complexity of ancient ceramic technology and to understand the potter, his craft, his guild, his family, and his town.

The cultural context of pottery manufacture is an area of investigation still in infancy. Two forms of scientific analysis show great promise in this nascent discipline. The first is neutron activation analysis, which provides an exact breakdown of the trace elements of the clay

> **Neutron activation analysis:** *scientific procedure that gives the exact breakdown of the trace elements of clay.*

used in pottery (Kaplan 1976). It can thus be determined whether the clay is of local manufacture (Perlman and Asaro 1969). Neutron activation was used, for example, on clay coffins found at Deir el-Balach. The coffins appeared to be related to Egyptian sarcophagi; accordingly, some archaeologists thought they might have come from Egypt. However, neutron activation analysis demonstrated that the clay was of local origin rather than having been imported from Egypt. As a result, archaeologists began searching for a local coffin-manufacturing installation.

The second scientific procedure is petrographic analysis, which entails microscopic examination of thin transparent sections of pottery (Amiran and Vroman 1946). This test gives data regarding the physical composition of the ceramic ware, that is, what type of clay was used,

> **Petrographic analysis:** *microscopic examination that provides data on the physical composition of clay.*

what temper, and so forth. The process requires sectioning of sherds into clean specimens for microscopic analysis.

Procedures for Excavating Pottery

As we have seen, archaeologists use pottery to date the strata of a mound and the artifacts discovered therein. They are successful, however, only if they collect the sherds and whole vessels in a controlled and systematic manner. If done in a haphazard fashion, pot-

Figure 7
The Development of Cooking Pots in Palestine

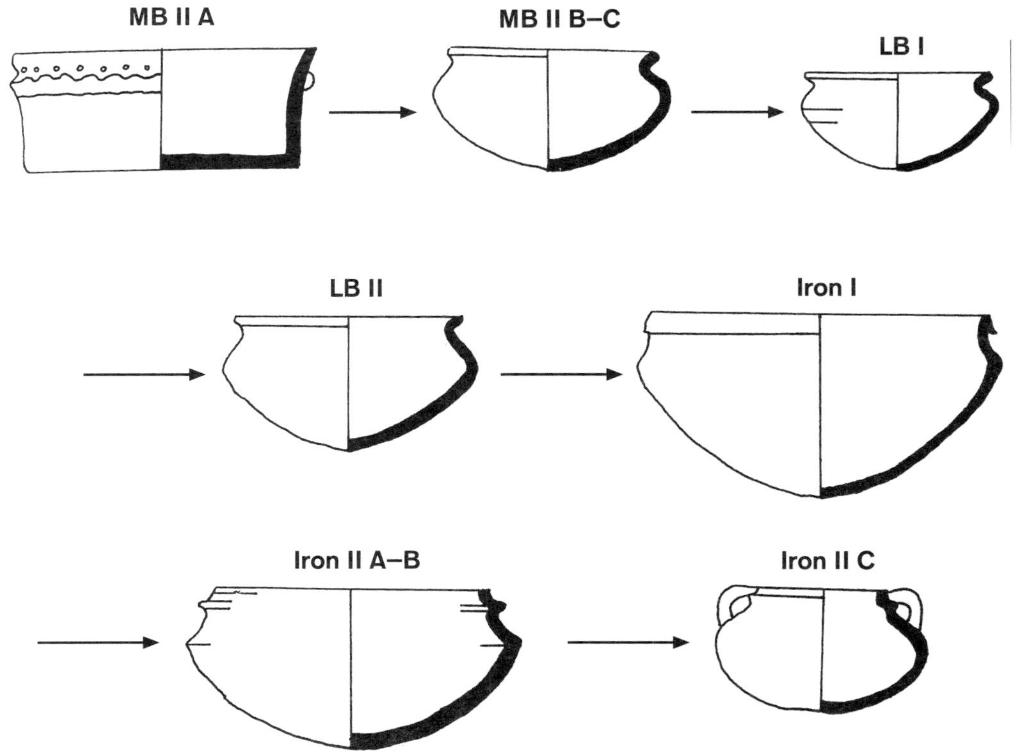

MB II A   MB II B–C   LB I

LB II   Iron I

Iron II A–B   Iron II C

tery collection is left open to intrusion, and any results are clearly suspect. Thus, proper organization of pottery gathering and reporting is critical to good archaeological technique (Blakely and Toombs 1981; Dever and Lance 1978; Seger 1971).

The first step is to dig up sherds and place them in a bucket. A tag on the bucket identifies the locus where the pottery was found. In addition, the archaeologist pinpoints the area of discovery on a top plan, thus ensuring proper correlation of the stratum, the locus, and the pottery. It should be noted that the date of a locus or stratum is determined by the latest sherd discovered in it (the terminus ad quem).

After excavation, the pottery is washed and then examined for inscriptions. Indicators and large body-sherds are brushed and allowed to dry. At the close of each excavation day, the archaeologist "reads" the pottery, primarily the indicator sherds, in order to date the locus. These sherds are marked with the locus number.

Sketches of the diagnostic sherds and whole vessels are drawn in the excavation's laboratory. They are represented in profile. For whole vessels, the left side of the illustration depicts the exterior appearance of the jar, while the right side represents the jar in section. Comparison of the drawings of pottery from different strata serves to indicate how forms have changed throughout history (see fig. 7). Clearly, if ceramic materials are excavated, handled, recorded, and illustrated properly, they can be of immense value in furthering our knowledge of biblical times.[3]

Bibliography

Albright, W. F. 1957. *From the Stone Age to Christianity*. 2d ed. Garden City, N.Y.: Doubleday.

———. 1971. *The Archaeology of Palestine*. Rev. ed. Gloucester, Mass.: Peter Smith.

Amiran, R. 1970. *Ancient Pottery of the Holy Land*. New Brunswick, N.J.: Rutgers University Press.

Amiran, R., and J. Vroman. 1946. "Petrographic Examination of Pottery." *BJPES* 12:10–15.

Blakely, J. A., and L. E. Toombs. 1981. *The Tell el-Hesi Field Manual*. Winona Lake, Ind.: Eisenbrauns.

Borowski, O. 1982. "Sherds, Sherds, Sherds." *BAR* 8.4:67–68.

———. 1988. "Ceramic Dating." In *Benchmarks in Time and Culture*, ed. J. F. Drinkard, G. L. Mattingly, and J. M. Miller, 223–33. Atlanta: Scholars.

Crowfoot, G. M. 1932. "Pots, Ancient and Modern." *PEFQS* 64:179–87.

Dever, W. G., and H. D. Lance, eds. 1978. *A Manual of Field Excavation: Handbook for Field Archaeologists*. Cincinnati: Hebrew Union College.

Di Vito, R. A. 1992. "Lachish Letters." *ABD* 4:126–28.

Glock, A. E. 1975. "Homo Faber: The Pot and the Potter at Taanach." *BASOR* 219:9–28.

Gonen, R. 1973. *Ancient Pottery*. London: Cassell.

Honeyman, A. M. 1939. "The Pottery Vessels of the Old Testament." *PEQ* 71:76–90.

Johnston, R. H. 1974. "The Biblical Potter." *BA* 37.4:86–106.

———. 1986. "Potter, Pottery." In *International Standard Bible Encyclopedia*, ed. G. W. Bromiley, 3:913–21. Grand Rapids: Eerdmans.

Kaplan, M. F. 1976. "Using Neutron Activation Analysis to Establish the Provenance of Pottery." *BAR* 2.1:30–32.

Kelso, J. L. 1948. *The Ceramic Vocabulary of the Old Testament*. New Haven: ASOR.

Lapp, P. W. 1961. *Palestinian Ceramic Chronology*. New Haven: ASOR.

———. 1975. *The Tale of the Tell*. Pittsburgh: Pickwick.

Matson, F. R., ed. 1965. *Ceramics and Man*. New York: Wenner-Gren.

Mazar, A. 1990. *Archaeology and the Land of the Bible*. New York: Doubleday.

Nicklin, K. 1971. "Stability and Innovation in Pottery Manufacture." *WA* 3:13–48.

Perlman, I., and F. Asaro. 1969. "Pottery Analysis by Neutron Activation." *Archaeometry* 11:21.

Petrie, W. M. F. 1891. *Tell el Hesy (Lachish)*. London: Watt.

Seger, J. 1971. *Handbook for Field Operations*. Jerusalem: Hebrew Union College.

Shepard, A. O. 1956. *Ceramics for the Archaeologist*. Washington, D.C.: Carnegie Institute.

Torczyner, H., et al. 1938. *Lachish I: The Lachish Letters*. London: Oxford University Press.

Wood, B. G. 1990. *The Sociology of Pottery in Ancient Palestine*. Sheffield, Eng.: JSOT.

Wright, G. E. 1937. *The Pottery of Palestine from the Earliest Times to the End of the Early Bronze Age*. New Haven: ASOR.

———. 1962. *Biblical Archaeology*. Philadelphia: Westminster.

Buildings

8

As excavation proceeds, the architectural features of a tell come to light. These features are commonly divided into two categories: buildings and fortifications. The former category is quite broad, including any man-made structures except fortifications: domestic, public, and sacred buildings. Fortifications include defensive structures like outer walls and gates. Our aim in this chapter is to examine the development of these two architectural categories during the history of ancient Palestine (Ben-Tor 1992; Frankfort 1954; Fritz 1995; Kempinski and Reich 1992).

For the most part, the architectural forms of Palestine are distinct from those of surrounding areas. At times, parallels can be drawn between Palestine and Mesopotamia or Egypt, but generally they cannot. In other words, there was some external influence on the architectural practices of ancient Palestine, yet it developed a building tradition of its own.

Temenos: *an enclosed sacred area for cultic practices.*

The major problem with attempting to define the architectural tradition of ancient Palestine is that there "are virtually no ancient buildings remaining above ground as standing monuments" (Wright 1985, 1:2). Archaeologists unearth ruins, often with only the foundations standing in situ. Because the buildings were destroyed, our ideas about elements such as roof design are frequently just speculation. Almost every reconstruction of an ancient building is theoretical, based upon ruined remains. Be that as it may, we can yet be assured that our understanding of ancient Palestine's architectural tradition is correct.

Early Bronze Age (c. 3200–2200 B.C.)

Domestic architecture. We begin our study of architecture with the Early Bronze Age because it is generally thought to be the first period of urbanization in Palestine and the period when tells begin to appear on a wide scale. In the early part of this period, curvilinear houses dominated. However, for most of the Early Bronze Age the principal form was the broad-room house. Among its characteristics were a single entrance in one of the long walls, benches along the inside walls, and a central post to support the roof. Many houses had a courtyard in the front. Excellent examples may be seen at the Negev site of Arad.

Sacred architecture. There was a great diversity of temple architecture in this period. For instance, two broad-room temples from Early Bronze Age II have been discovered at Megiddo. They were attached to and flanked an altar. A wall encircled the whole sacred area *(temenos)*. These temples were followed in Early Bronze III by a series of sacred shrines called megaron temples, each of which had an antechamber. In Area T at Arad two buildings connected by a common wall have been dubbed the Twin Temples. One of the rooms contained a raised platform *(bāmāh)* and a stone-lined basin, both probably used for cultic purposes. A monumental temple with a wall surrounding the sacred precinct has been found on the acropolis of Ai.

Public architecture. A few palaces have been discovered, the most notable being the elaborate Palace 3177 at Megiddo. Another most intriguing public building of the period was the charnel house, examples of which

Bāmāh: *a raised platform or "high place" used for cultic worship.*

have been found at Megiddo and Bab edh Dhra. These buildings served as repositories for the bones of secondary burials. Their design was very similar to the broad-room domestic residence of the time. There are, however, a few examples that were circular in plan.

A unique public structure was the circular granary. Found in clusters at Khirbet Kerak and Arad, these buildings were shaped like beehives and measured twelve to twenty-four feet in diameter. Presumably men poured grain in at the top of the beehive through a trap door, and the grain was extracted at the bottom through a similar trap door (Currid 1985 and 1986).

> Charnel house: *a room or building used as a repository for secondary burials of human bones.*

Fortifications. Defensive systems during the Early Bronze Age were bigger and heavier than any previous fortifications. The plan at Arad is a prime example. The outer wall which surrounded the site was about eight feet thick and extended for two-thirds of a mile, enclosing twenty-two acres. Every sixty to eighty feet (depending on the contours of the tell) a semicircular bastion was built into the outer wall. These towers measured ten to twelve feet in diameter. One entered the bastion through a doorway in the city wall. Entry into the city was through postern gates that measured no more than three to four feet wide.

There was a similarity of design throughout Palestine in the Early Bronze Age. The glacis, a man-made sloping revetment used to protect the base of a tell's outer fortification wall, may have made its first appearance in Palestine at this time.

> Postern gate: *a narrow opening that serves as a subsidiary entrance in town walls.*

Middle Bronze Age (c. 2200–1550 B.C.)

The transition between Early Bronze and Middle Bronze was quite dramatic. The main regions of habitation changed to arid areas, particularly the central Negev and Sinai. Architecture in the transition was meager, demonstrating a stark shift from Early Bronze buildings. For example, instead of the broad-room house common in the Early Bronze Age, dwellings now consisted of a single rounded chamber, very small, with a stone pillar at the center to hold up a roof of stone. It was not until the second half of the

Middle Bronze Age that a highly developed architectural tradition emerged (Daviau 1993).

Domestic architecture. As we have seen, the broad-room design of the Early Bronze Age gave way to small round chambers. Midway through the Middle Bronze Age, however, houses became multiroomed complexes built around a central hall or court. Most also had a second story.

Sacred architecture. The tradition of the broad-room temple continued into the Middle Bronze Age, examples of which include rectangular structures found at Hazor (Area A) and at Ebla (Mazar 1990, 212). The primary modification in temple design during this period was the appearance of Migdol temples. These were monumental square or rectangular structures with two massive towers at the entrance. The best examples have been unearthed at Shechem and Megiddo.

Public architecture. Several palatial structures from the Middle Bronze Age have been excavated (at least partially) in Palestine. Some, like the examples from Megiddo, were large architectural complexes. One of the buildings at Megiddo contained two courts and ten to twenty subsidiary rooms. Although not large by ancient Near Eastern standards, such structures were impressive in the context of Palestine.

In addition, town planning became more defined than in the Early Bronze Age. "It may be hazarded that as a minimum there was a continuous way around the periphery of the tell and that each sector, quarter or division was served by at least one street offering direct access to this peripheral way. . . . Within the terms of its layout the significant difference from the EB period in the over-all aspect of the city was that in this later period the towns were much more densely occupied and thus building development was more closely packed together" (Wright 1985, 1:55).

Fortifications. During Middle Bronze II, the defenses of tells became quite large and elaborate. Most of the cities were now surrounded by immense solid outer walls. At Gezer, for example, a twelve-foot-wide wall encircled the city. Entrances into the city through the walls were provided by enormous multichambered gates, a Middle Bronze innovation. The gate at Gezer included two mud-brick towers that aided in the defense of the city. Another prime example was the vaulted mud-brick gate at Tell Dan. The arch was an improvement over the previous styles, which, being flat and made largely of timbers, could be more easily destroyed. The gate, of course, was the most vulnerable spot in an ancient city and had to be protected. The gate at Tell Dan was more secure than most because a pavement with stone steps led up to it. That design denied chariots, battering rams, and other vehicles of war access to the gate.

The glacis was widely employed in Middle Bronze fortifications. Hazor, the largest tell in Palestine at the time (180–200 acres), had a glacis surrounding the lower city and another one encircling its acropolis. The arched gateway at Tell Dan was joined to a glacis on both sides. Moats also appeared for the first time. At both Acco and Achzib a glacis and a moat were used together.

Late Bronze Age (c. 1550–1200 b.c.)

A great decline in the number of populated sites occurred in the first part of the Late Bronze Age. There does not appear to have been any population break at the time, but many sites were abandoned. Some cities were destroyed by Egyptian raids. In the latter half of the Late Bronze Age, however, many of the sites that had been abandoned were resettled, such as Tell Beit Mirsim and Jericho. Because of the apparent continuity of the population from Middle Bronze into Late Bronze, many of the architectural forms remained the same or were similar.

Domestic architecture. The basic Late Bronze house consisted of a central courtyard surrounded by rooms on several sides. The design and proportions of the rooms appear to have varied. This house style, first seen in the Middle Bronze Age, continued into and dominated the Late Bronze Age. Large patrician houses have been discovered at Megiddo, Taanach, and Aphek (Mazar 1990, 246). They consisted of a large central courtyard encircled by good-sized rooms and hallways.

Sacred architecture. Just as with domestic dwellings, a close association is evident between the designs of Middle and Late Bronze temple structures. Some of the major temples were originally built in the Middle Bronze Age, and then rebuilt or renovated in the Late Bronze. Good examples have been found at Hazor (Temple H) and at Megiddo (Tower Temple). The latter was first constructed in Middle Bronze II and did not go out of use until the twelfth century B.C., a period covering about five hundred years.

There was a great variety in the design of Late Bronze temples. The main type seems to have been a monumental broad-room structure. The entrance led from a porch into the main hall. The most sacred part of the temple was located in the main hall opposite the entrance. The building design was symmetrical. Temple H at Hazor and the Tower Temple at Megiddo follow this pattern.

Examples of irregular temple plans are numerous. The fosse temples at Lachish were constructed outside the tell within the old Middle Bronze moat that had surrounded the city. These temples all had a bent entrance that was near the end of one of the long walls and led into a main hall. In the main hall were an altar and benches. The roof was supported by a series of wooden columns.

> Bent entrance: *an entrance near the end of one of the long walls of a rectangular room or building.*

Public architecture. Undoubtedly the most notable Late Bronze palace complex was at Megiddo. Its design was in essence like the old Middle Bronze palace at the site: a series of rooms around a central courtyard. The Megiddo complex evolved gradually from a square structure in the sixteenth century to a rectangular one in the fourteenth century. The main difference between this building and Middle Bronze palaces was its massive walls. The building was destroyed in the thirteenth century.

Fortifications. Curiously, sites of the Late Bronze Age had almost a complete lack of defensive systems. No city walls have been uncovered at such major tells as Megiddo and Lachish. Towns that did have some fortifications, like Hazor, merely copied the plans of the previous Middle Bronze systems.

Iron Age (1200–586 B.C.)

Because of the vast amounts of material from the Iron Age, it is necessary to divide it into two parts: Iron Age I (1200–1000 B.C.) and Iron Age II (1000–586 B.C.). From a sociopolitical perspective this is an appropriate division because in the earlier period Israel was a loose tribal confederation, in the later, a monarchy.

Iron Age I (1200–1000 b.c.)

Domestic architecture. A distinctive type of house became common in Iron Age I. The four-room house was a rectangular design with the entrance on one

> **Four-room house:** *a rectangular residence with three parallel long rooms and a broad room at the rear.*

of the short sides. Inside were four rooms, three parallel long rooms and a broad room at the rear (Shiloh 1970). Rows of pillars divided the house into rooms and probably supported the roof. While these structures are often referred to as Israelite four-room houses, that is too narrow a designation because they were also found in Philistine contexts during the Iron Age. In addition, the four-room plan appears to have had antecedents in the Bronze Age prior to Israel's occupation of the land.

Sacred architecture. Temples are unknown in Israelite contexts from Iron Age I. However, some scholars believe that they have discovered the remains of religious shrines (not temples). Adam Zertal (1985), for instance, has proposed that an Israelite shrine existed on Mount Ebal. His proposal has not received wide acceptance (Kempinski 1986).

Major temple complexes have been discovered at Tell Qasile, which was under Philistine control at the time. Three successive temples were built on the same site between 1150 and 1000 b.c. Another sanctuary was found at Sarepta, a Phoenician port near the northern border of Israel.

Public architecture/fortifications. Monumental buildings such as palaces are almost completely missing from Israelite settlements of the period. The typical Israelite site was a small village containing clusters of four-room houses and little else. "The picture we get in these early Israelite hill-country villages is of a very simple, rather impoverished, somewhat isolated culture with no great artistic or architectural tradition behind it" (Dever 1992, 42). A majority of these villages were unfortified and had no outer city wall. The only exceptions appear to have been Har Adir and Giloh, where have been discovered, respectively, a square fortress and a tall, fortified tower. Houses may have been clustered together at some sites, such as 'Izbet Sartah, to afford protection for the entire community (Finkelstein 1988, 76).

The circumstances at sites under Philistine control were far different. For example, large palaces have been found at Tell Miqne and perhaps at Tell Qasile. Many Philistine cities were strongly fortified. Massive city walls have been revealed at Ashdod and Ekron. Town planning and city development were far more advanced at Philistine sites than at their Israelite counterparts.

Miscellaneous features. It was during Iron Age I that the practice of agricultural terracing began in the mountainous areas of Palestine (de Geus 1975; Ron 1966; Stager 1982). This new technique allowed the farmer to cultivate previously untouched ground. A good example occurred at Khirbet Raddanah (Callaway and Cooley 1971).

Grain storage pits were numerous during Iron Age I (Currid and Navon 1989). At Taanach, for instance, "in SW 1–9 alone there was evidence of some 17 pits, most of them quite deep, cut in the 12th century B.C." (Lapp 1969, 34). Similar conditions existed at the tells of Shechem and Hazor.

Iron Age II (1000–586 B.C.)

Domestic architecture. Houses continued to follow the four-room pattern that first appeared widely in Iron Age I (Shiloh 1970 and 1987). Some of the houses, however, contained only three rooms, although they were clearly a variation of the four-room plan. Many of the houses were two-storied (Stager 1985).

Sacred architecture. There are no remains of Solomon's temple in Jerusalem. Many scholars believe that it was located on the site of the platform that today houses the El-Aqsa Mosque and the Dome of the Rock. Detailed dimensions and plans of the Hebrew temple are recorded in 1 Kings 6 and 2 Chronicles 3–4. The layout of the sacred shrine was quite similar to a later temple (eighth century B.C.) at Tell Tainat in northern Syria.

A ritual center from the ninth century B.C. has been uncovered at Tell Dan. It consists of a square enclosure with a podium inside (possibly for a temple on top) and a sacrificial altar. This sacred area is probably what remains of what Jeroboam I erected at the site of Dan (1 Kings 12). At the extreme other end of Palestine a hewn ashlar altar from the late eighth or early seventh century B.C. was discovered at Beersheba.

The only Iron Age temple found in Judah was unearthed at Arad (in the Iron Age fortress). It has three sections: a courtyard, a broad room, and an inner sanctuary. Two standing stones and two incense altars leading into the sanctuary suggest that some type of deviant Hebrew religion was practiced here.

Public architecture. Monumental architecture from Iron Age II is abundant in Israel. At Megiddo, for example, two palaces have been identified (1723 and 6000). Their design is similar to the Syro-Hittite *bit hilani* structure that consists of a pillared entrance, central courtyard, and surrounding rectangular rooms. A palace recently discovered at Bethsaida has a similar design.

At Lachish a massive podium (the largest block of masonry in Palestine) supported two large palaces. Nothing remains of the palaces, although their design is evident from the foundation. One is similar to the Megiddo palaces in having a central courtyard and surrounding storerooms.

A palace reminiscent of Ahab's "ivory house" (1 Kings 22:39) was found at Samaria. Numerous and costly ivory articles were found in the debris of the building. A small palace at Ramat Rahel consisted of two buildings surrounded by storerooms.

Buildings with three long rooms divided by two rows of pillars (thus the term "tripartite pillared buildings") appear at several major tells: Megiddo, Hazor, and Beersheba. The purpose of these structures has been greatly debated. Some believe they are stables, others storehouses, and still others markets (Currid 1993).

> **Tripartite pillared building:** *a public structure that has three long rooms divided by two rows of pillars.*

A large public silo from the eighth or seventh century was uncovered in Area A at Megiddo. With a diameter of eleven meters at the top and seven meters at the bottom, the silo was seven meters deep. A pair of winding stairs (a unique feature of the Iron Age silos) presumably allowed the grain to be deposited and extracted manually.

Some contend that a large structure with stone steps that was discovered in recent excavations in Jerusalem is the *millo* (literally "filling") mentioned in 1 Kings 9:15. Others insist the *millo* was stone terracing on the Ophel Hill (Stager 1982).

Fortifications. Defensive systems displayed great variety in Iron Age II. For example, there was no dominant style in the construction of outer walls. In the tenth century, casemate walls protected Gezer and Hazor, but a solid wall surrounded Chinnereth. During the ninth and eighth centuries Beth Shemesh had a casemate wall, Lachish a solid wall, Tell en-Nasbeh an offset-inset wall, and Rabud a zigzag wall. This great diversity lasted into the sixth century B.C. (Herr 1997, 126, 144, 157–58).

Most gates in early Iron Age II had six chambers; those in the middle of that period were built smaller and contained only four chambers. But that did not always hold true: during most of Iron Age II the gates of Gezer had two chambers, Beersheba four, and 'Ira six.

A few settlements were strictly fortresses (Aharoni 1967; Cohen 1979). The best example was Arad. At Jezreel a moat and a rampart were constructed around the tell. Along the top of the tell was a large casemate wall. Such heavy fortifications appear to have been a rarity in Iron Age II.

Building Materials and Styles

A key factor in the development of architecture is the type of building materials that are available (Rapoport 1969, 24–28). People use what is accessible. In the southwestern United States, for example, the principal construction material has always been adobe (sun-dried brick). While other factors, such as tradition, religion, and climate, play a role, the availability of building materials stands at the top of the list.

Mud-brick: *a common building material consisting of mud and straw (or other temper).*

One of the most available building materials in Palestine is mud-brick. It has been employed there throughout history, even to the present day. Often the natural clay was mixed with an element like straw, put in a mold, and then allowed to dry and harden in the sun. Some bricks seem to have been fired to strengthen them and to make them fireproof.

The earliest mud-brick structures in Palestine were erected at Jericho in the prepottery Neolithic A period (8th millennium B.C.).

The bricks are often referred to as hog-backed because they had a curved upper surface and a flat base. In the subsequent pre-pottery Neolithic B period (c. 7000 B.C.) the shape of the

> **Hog-backed bricks:** *mud-bricks with a flat base and a curved upper surface.*

bricks at Jericho changed: they now were cigar-shaped. In the Early Bronze Age the mud-bricks took on rectangular and square forms that became standardized for the remaining history of Palestine.

Mud-brick construction was practiced concurrently with other building techniques. During the Early Bronze Age it was common for the foundation or base of a wall to consist of a few rows of boulders held together with mortar. On top of it were layers of mud-brick, one row staggering another. Mortar was often used with the mud-brick as well.

Many structures were built with stone. Good stone for construction was freely available in most parts of Palestine, in particular, limestone and basalt. Some buildings and walls were simply erected out of fieldstones

> **Ashlar masonry:** *finely dressed blocks that have been cut rectangularly and may be set with mortar.*

that had been gathered from around a site. Other installations were built with stones that had been cut and dressed in a precise manner. One technique of wall construction was to set large, unhewn field boulders into place and then fill in the openings with small fieldstones. Sometimes walls were built in double rows with rubble placed between them.

One of the characteristic building techniques during the Iron Age was ashlar masonry. This heavily dressed stone was often arranged in header-stretcher fashion. That is, courses of stones whose shorter ends were exposed (headers) alternated with courses whose longer ends were exposed (stretchers). By Hellenistic times there was frequently a raised, undressed face (boss).

There were many other styles of wall construction. It is important to note that wall design and form are not good indicators of chronology. Many of the building methods were employed by various groups over a wide area and lengthy time span. Therefore, one needs to be careful in assigning a particular technique to a particular time period. It is better to use pottery to resolve chronological issues.

Bibliography

Aharoni, Y. 1967. "Forerunners of the Limes: Iron Age Fortresses in the Negev." *IEJ* 17:1–17.

Ben-Tor, A., ed. 1992. *The Archaeology of Ancient Israel*. New Haven: Yale University Press.

Callaway, J. A., and R. E. Cooley. 1971. "A Salvage Excavation at Raddana, in Bireh." *BASOR* 201:9–19.

Cohen, R. 1979. "The Iron Age Fortresses in the Central Negev." *BASOR* 236:61–79.

Currid, J. 1985. "The Beehive Granaries of Ancient Palestine." *ZDPV* 101:151–64.

———. 1986. "The Beehive Buildings of Ancient Palestine." *BA* 49.1:20–24.

———. 1993. "Rectangular Storehouse Construction during the Israelite Iron Age." *ZDPV* 108:99–121.

Currid, J., and A. Navon. 1989. "Iron Age Pits and the Lahav (Tel Halif) Grain Storage Project." *BASOR* 273:67–78.

Daviau, M. 1993. *Houses and Their Furnishings in Bronze Age Palestine: Domestic Activity Areas and Artifact Distribution in the Middle and Late Bronze Ages*. Sheffield, Eng.: JSOT.

Dever, W. G. 1992. "How to Tell a Canaanite from an Israelite." In H. Shanks et al., *The Rise of Ancient Israel*, 27–56. Washington, D.C.: Biblical Archaeological Society.

Finkelstein, I. 1988. *The Archaeology of the Israelite Settlement*. Jerusalem: Israel Exploration Society.

Frankfort, H. 1954. *The Art and Architecture of the Ancient Orient*. Baltimore: Penguin.

Fritz, V. 1995. *The City in Ancient Israel*. Sheffield, Eng.: Sheffield Academic Press.

de Geus, C. H. J. 1975. "The Importance of Archaeological Research into the Palestinian Agricultural Terraces with an Excursus on the Word *gbi*." *PEQ* 107:65–74.

Herr, L. 1997. "The Iron II Period: Emerging Nations." *BA* 60.3:114–83.

Kempinski, A. 1986. "Joshua's Altar—An Iron Age I Watchtower." *BAR* 12.1:42–49.

Kempinski, A., and R. Reich, eds. 1992. *The Architecture of Ancient Israel*. Jerusalem: Israel Exploration Society.

Lapp, P. W. 1969. "The 1968 Excavations at Tell Ta'annek." *BASOR* 195:2–49.

Mazar, A. 1990. *Archaeology of the Land of the Bible*. New York: Doubleday.

Rapoport, A. 1969. *House Form and Culture*. Englewood Cliffs, N.J.: Prentice-Hall.

Ron, Z. 1966. "Agricultural Terraces in the Judean Mountains." *IEJ* 16:33–49, 111–22.

Shiloh, Y. 1970. "The Four-Room House: Its Situation and Function in the Israelite City." *IEJ* 20:180–90.

———. 1987. "The Casemate Wall, the Four-Room House, and Early Planning in the Israelite City." *BASOR* 268:3–15.

Stager, L. E. 1982. "The Archaeology of the East Slope of Jerusalem and the Terraces of Kidron." *JNES* 41:111–21.

———. 1985. "Archaeology of the Family in Ancient Israel." *BASOR* 260:1–35.

Wright, G. R. H. 1985. *Ancient Building in South Syria and Palestine.* 2 vols. Leiden: Handbuch der Orientalistik.

Zertal, A. 1985. "Has Joshua's Altar Been Found on Mt. Ebal?" *BAR* 11.1:26–43.

Small Finds 9

One of the great moments in a digger's life is discovering an ancient object that may be held in one's hand. Imagine finding a denarius at a New Testament site such as Capernaum or Bethsaida, the type of coin that Jesus used in his confrontation with the religious leaders in Mark 12:13–17. Or uncovering an iron spearhead used in Babylonia's destruction of Jerusalem in 586 B.C. Or being the first to see Hebrew writing on pottery or parchment that has been hidden for thousands of years. These are just a few examples of small finds—they are discovered almost every day on a dig and therefore constitute important pieces of the archaeological puzzle.

Let us begin by defining the term "small find." A small find is any man-made object that is discovered on or in a tell but is not architecture or pottery. Ceramic is often considered a small find, but we treat it separately primarily because of its chronological

> **Small find:** *any man-made object that is discovered in an excavation but is not architecture or pottery.*

value. Of course, the types of small finds vary from site to site, depending upon factors such as the site's subsistence base, the natural resources in the area, trade, and so forth. Our discussion will categorize small finds according to the material from which they were primarily made. The five basic categories are metalwork, stonework, bonework, woodwork, and glassware.

Metalwork

The history of metallurgy in the ancient Near East is quite complex and beset with numerous chronological difficulties. Therefore what we present here is only a basic outline of the development of metalwork in the Fertile Crescent. The first metal to be used appears to have been native copper. During the Neolithic period (eighth millennium B.C.) it was "fashioned into small decorative pins and pendants, a phase that has aptly been called trinket metallurgy" (Craddock 1996, 461).

The mining and smelting industries did not come on the scene until the fifth and fourth millennia B.C. (Levy 1987, 357–71; 1990, 27). Gold and silver began to be used at this time, both primarily in jewelry. Bronze, an alloy of copper and tin, was not commonly used until the early third millennium B.C. Iron was discovered as early as the end of the third millennium, but was not put to great use until the latter stages of the second. Bronze and iron were used in a variety of ways throughout the history of Palestine.

1. *Coinage* (Kindler and Stein 1987; Kreitzer 1996; Meshorer 1982). Coins may be defined as minted metal that serves as money or a medium of exchange. It is likely that the first coins were struck in the late seventh and early sixth centuries B.C. in western Asia Minor (Betlyon 1992, 1078). Not many coins have been found from Iron Age Palestine. Coin minting and circulation did not really take place there until after the fall of Jerusalem. Coins from the latter stages of the Persian age bear the name *Yehud* (i.e., Judea). They were probably struck at or near Jerusalem.

2. *Weapons* (Yadin 1963). Metal weapons were rare in Palestine into the Early Bronze Age. Those that have been discovered, such as the Kfar Monash hoard, were all copper. Although sparse, the basic weapons—daggers, axes, and spears—are well represented.

The same types of weapons appeared in the transition to the Middle Bronze Age, only now some were made out of bronze. Middle Bronze II weaponry was almost all bronze, and a few new types were produced. These included duckbill axeheads and ridged daggers. The weapons of the Late Bronze Age were similar to those of the Middle Bronze, although use increased dramatically. During Iron Age I, while the basic design remained much the same, the transition was made from bronze to iron as the main metal in weapons (Muhly 1982).

3. *Tools.* The earliest tools of the ancient Near East were chopping instruments made of rock (Braidwood 1975, 50). Not until the Chalcolithic period did tools of copper appear, and not until the latter stages did they become common. At Beersheba (Abu Matar) a copper adze was uncovered from the Chalcolithic levels. In addition, twenty chisels were among the four hundred copper objects discovered in the Cave of the Treasure at Nahal Mishmar.

Although metal tools (copper and bronze) from the Bronze Age have been found at many sites, it was not until the Iron Age that metal tools, which were particularly important in agriculture, were universally employed. The introduction of iron **Cave of the Treasure: *a cache of Chalcolithic copper and ivory artifacts found at Nahal Mishmar.*** made for stronger tools; for example, bronze plows snapped easily in the ground, but iron ones did not. On the other hand, the replacement of stone sickles by metal ones was a relatively late development in Palestine. Even into the early parts of the Iron Age, Palestinian farmers continued to reap their crops with flint sickles, as did their Neolithic predecessors (Gonen 1979, 30). Also worth mention is that fishing equipment often consisted of a metal base. Of particular note is the gear discovered at the New Testament fishing village of Bethsaida.

In the Roman period the use of metal tools expanded considerably. Found in all fields of work, Roman tools were so well manufactured that it is difficult to distinguish them from many modern tools.

4. *Jewelry.* One of the earliest uses of metal in Palestine was for human adornment. Copper beads from the Chalcolithic period appear to have been the earliest usage of metal at Tell Abu Matar. Copper armlets and what may have been a crown were part of the Nahal Mishmar horde (Cave of the Treasure) from the same period. These metal objects were probably for ceremonial rather than secular use.

The earliest example of gold jewelry to come to light was discovered in a tomb in Galilee from Early Bronze Age II. It was a round gold plaque with a pierced center and decoration in relief. However, it was not until the Late Bronze Age that metal jewelry became widespread in Palestine. Most impressive is the collection of gold jewelry discovered at Tell el-Ajjul from the beginning of the Late Bronze Age. Included are gold and silver earrings, bracelets, an eight-pointed star, and various amulets. Pendants with representations of the goddess Astarte are also part of the collection. By contrast, metal jewelry from the Iron Age is rare and simply or even crudely manufactured.

Stonework

> Flake: *a small piece or chip removed from a large piece of rock or other natural material in order to produce a tool.*

The earliest small finds related to human culture are stone tools used to gather and prepare food. Naturally occurring rocks were modified for use as implements. "The modification of an original, unworked piece of stone that produces any kind of chipped stone tool is always done by striking off or otherwise removing smaller pieces from the original larger piece. The general term for the smaller fragments so removed is *flake*; the larger piece is usually called a *core*" (Braidwood 1975, 41). Among the various tools made from stone are choppers, scrapers, hammers, axes, cleavers, and knives.

Other ancient artifacts like figurines, cookware, ovens, and grinding implements (e.g., mortars and pestles) were also often made of stone. In addition, stone was used for jewelry. At Beidha a Neolithic factory (c. 7000 B.C.) produced stone, shell, and bone beads.

> Core: *a large stone or other natural material from which flakes were removed in order to produce tools.*

Stonework naturally declined when metal became available to the ancients during the Bronze Age. In prehistoric archaeology stonework plays a major role. During the Iron Age, however, stone implements, though still used, no longer dominated physical culture.

Bonework

Bonework appeared later than stonework. The ancients used bone for a variety of tools. "There are knives, pins, needles with eyes, and little double-pointed straight bars of bone, called *gorges*, that were probably used for catching fish" (Braidwood 1975, 76). Bone picks are among the discoveries at early sites like Jisr Banat Yaaquv and El Wad.

Jewelry was another use for bone. It has been found in the form of beads, pendants, and necklaces. Bracelets and necklaces of dentalium have been recovered. Bone was employed as well for figurines and idols. Recent excavations at Ashkelon have revealed an extensive bone industry at the site (Wapnish 1991).

> Dentalium: *a genus of mollusks with an open-coned shell used for beads.*

Woodwork

The importance of wood in the development of societies in the ancient Near East should not be overlooked. As the primary agent of fuel in antiquity (either as wood or charcoal), it was essential to the development of many crafts, trades, and arts (Taylor 1996, 758). Cooking, metalworking, and pottery making required wood for fuel. Numerous tools had wooden handles: hammers, axes, and plows.

The major problem with wood for archaeology is decay. In Palestine it has survived almost exclusively in the arid atmosphere of the Dead Sea area, such as in a few tombs at Jericho "where even dessicated joints of meat still lay on the original wooden dishes. These tombs were cut in limestone and then walled up after the burials had been made. Carbon monoxide and methane gas seeping into closed tombs through cracks in the rock replaced the normal air that would have allowed bacteria to live. Consequently organic materials have survived" (Moorey 1981, 98).

Wood may also be preserved in conditions of extreme wetness. Excavations at Carthage (Tunisia), for example, seem to have uncovered a fragment of a wooden log from the cofferdam used in building the city's quay. Similarly, a boat submerged in the muddy basin of the Sea of Galilee was preserved for two thousand years (Wachsmann 1988).

Glassware

Glass first appeared in Palestine in a natural state called obsidian. Obsidian is a natural glass resulting from the quick cooling of lava. The examples found from the Neolithic and Chalcolithic periods were not native to Palestine, but were probably imported from Anatolia in the north.

Man-made glass was produced by fusion of various raw materials, normally including silicates, soda, and lime. Often it also contained potash and lead oxide. The earliest artificial glass, which was in the form of beads for jewelry, appeared simultaneously in Egypt and Mesopotamia at the beginning of the third millennium B.C.

The first glass vessel was not produced until the middle of the second millennium (c. 1600 B.C.), and this also occurred in both Egypt and Mesopotamia. Several Palestinian sites, notably Lachish and Beth Shean, have yielded glass vessels from the fourteenth and thirteenth centuries B.C.

Glass blowing did not begin until the Roman period. With that innovation glass objects became ubiquitous at Roman sites. Jerusalem had a major glass factory at the time (Avigad 1983).

Many of the topics we have briefly surveyed require study by specialists. Professionals in the areas of palaeosteology, palaeobotany, palaeoethnology, geology, geography, and many other fields of research, are now a necessary part of the archaeological project. The field archaeologist simply cannot master all of the disciplines. Long gone are the days when the archaeologist did all the work alone. With the great explosion of information we must rely upon those who specialize in particular areas of research.

Bibliography

Avigad, N. 1983. "Jerusalem Flourishing—A Craft Center for Stone, Pottery and Glass." *BAR* 9.6:48–65.

Betlyon, J. 1992. "Coinage." *ABD* 1:1076–89.

Braidwood, R. J. 1975. *Prehistoric Men.* 8th ed. Glenview, Ill.: Scott, Foresman.

Craddock, P. T. 1996. "Metallurgy in the Old World." In *The Oxford Companion to Archaeology,* ed. B. Fagan, 461–62. New York: Oxford University Press.

Gonen, R. 1979. *Grain*. Jerusalem: Shikmona.

Kindler, A., and A. Stein. 1987. *A Bibliography of the City Coinage of Palestine*. Oxford: British Archaeological Reports.

Kreitzer, L. J. 1996. *Striking New Images: Roman Imperial Coinage and the New Testament World*. Sheffield, Eng.: Sheffield Academic Press.

Levy, T., ed. 1987. *Shiqmim I*. Oxford: British Archaeological Reports.

Levy, T. 1990. "Craft Specialization First Appears in the Chalcolithic Period." *BAR* 16.6:27.

Meshorer, Y. 1982. *Ancient Jewish Coinage*. Dix Hills, N.Y.: Amphora.

Moorey, P. R. S. 1981. *Excavation in Palestine*. Guildford, Eng.: Lutterworth.

Muhly, J. D. 1982. "How Iron Age Technology Changed the Ancient World—and Gave the Philistines a Military Edge." *BAR* 8.6:40–54.

Taylor, M. 1996. "Wood." In *The Oxford Companion to Archaeology*, ed. B. Fagan, 758–59. New York: Oxford University Press.

Wachsmann, S. 1988. "The Galilee Boat—2,000-Year-Old Hull Recovered Intact." *BAR* 14.5:18–33.

Wapnish, P. 1991. "Beauty and Utility in Bone—New Light on Bone Crafting." *BAR* 17.4:54–57.

Yadin, Y. 1963. *The Art of Warfare in Biblical Lands in the Light of Archaeological Study*. 2 vols. New York: McGraw-Hill.

Archaeology in Use: The Recovery of Bethsaida 10

Our final chapter presents an example of the archaeological process from beginning to end at one site. Although several sites could be analyzed, we have selected the site of Bethsaida as the focus of our study. The reasons for choosing this tell are threefold:

1. The excavation of Bethsaida offers concrete, specific examples of each of the archaeological procedures examined in this book.
2. Full-scale digging at the tell did not begin until 1988, and continues vigorously today. It thus employs the most up-to-date methods and techniques of excavation and analysis.
3. The author has firsthand knowledge of the site, having excavated there three times, including service as a field archaeologist in 1997 (Field A).

Site Identification

Bethsaida is mentioned frequently in the New Testament Gospel accounts. These records indicate that it was a port city on the northern shore of the Sea of Galilee (Mark 6:45). That it was located in the district of Galilee is confirmed by its name "Bethsaida of Galilee"

(John 12:21). Bethsaida was the hometown of at least three disciples: Andrew, Peter, and Philip (John 1:44), all apparently fishermen by occupation. Bethsaida played a significant role in Jesus' Galilean ministry. There he healed a blind man (Mark 8:22–25) and performed numerous other miracles (Matt. 11:21). Perhaps the feeding of the five thousand occurred nearby (Luke 9:10–17). Alongside Chorazin, Jesus cursed Bethsaida as a city of unbelief and unrepentance (Luke 10:13).

The Jewish historian Flavius Josephus mentions Bethsaida a few times in his writings of the first century A.D. (Rousseau and Arav 1995, 20). Josephus reports that after the death of Herod the Great in 4 B.C., Bethsaida was subsumed into the tetrarchy of Philip, Herod's son (*Antiquities* 17.189). In A.D. 30 Philip honored the town by proclaiming it a polis and renaming it Julias: Philip elevated the village of "Bethsaida on Lake Genesaritis [Galilee] to the status of a city by adding residents and strengthening fortifications. He named it after Julia, the emperor's daughter" (*Antiquities* 18.2.1 [28]). (Evidence shows that it was actually renamed after Livia-Julia, mother of the emperor Tiberius [Kuhn and Arav 1991, 87–90].) Finally, Josephus describes a major battle of the Jewish War (A.D. 66–73) that occurred near Bethsaida. There the Jewish rebels fought against the forces of Agrippa II, apparently to a draw.

Very little about Bethsaida is found in the rabbinic sources from the first to third centuries A.D. (Freund 1995, 302). We do know, however, that the site was a place of pilgrimage for the early church. In A.D. 530 Theodosius commented: "From Seven Springs (Tabgha) it is two miles to Capernaum. From Capernaum it is six miles to Bethsaida, where the Apostles Peter, Andrew, Philip, and the sons of Zebedee were born. From Bethsaida it is fifty miles to Panias: that is the place where the Jordan rises from the two places Ior and Dan" (Wilkinson 1977, 63). The pilgrim Willibald visited Bethsaida in 725: "From there [Capernaum, Willibald and his companions] went to Bethsaida, the city of Peter and Andrew: there is now a church there in the place where originally their house stood" (Wilkinson 1977, 128; Pixner 1985, 208).

Over the course of time, the exact location of Bethsaida was lost. A dispute arose regarding this matter in the year 1590 (Rousseau and Arav 1995, 20). The Dutch scholar Adrichomius argued that Julias and Bethsaida were two different sites, one located on the east and the other on the west of the Jordan River. Some support for that interpretation emerged during the next half century.[1] Others, however, such as John Lightfoot, held to the position that the Gospels and Josephus refer to the same city (Rousseau and Arav 1995, 20).

With the rise of modern archaeological research, the question of Bethsaida's location came to the fore. The American researcher Edward Robinson visited the area in 1838, and he too claimed that there were two Bethsaidas: Julias Bethsaida was at the site called et-Tell, and Bethsaida Galilee was located at Tabgha (Smith 1993, 5). The German archaeologist Gottlieb Schumacher, a half century later, disagreed with Robinson because et-Tell is 1.25 miles north of the Sea of Galilee. How could it be a fishing village if it was not next to the sea? So he advanced two other sites for consideration: el-Araj and Mesadiye, both located on the Sea of Galilee east of the Jordan River.

In the twentieth century, attention focused on two sites, et-Tell and el-Araj. El-Araj is a low mound measuring ten thousand square meters and located one mile to the east of the Jordan River where it runs into the Sea of Galilee. Numerous modern scholars have identified it as Bethsaida (Avi-Yonah 1977, 105). The site of et-Tell is much higher and larger than el-Araj: it covers some eighty thousand square meters and rises twenty-five meters above the surrounding plain. Few modern scholars have identified et-Tell with Bethsaida because of its distance from the Sea of Galilee.

In order to help solve the problem, Rami Arav sunk probes at both sites in 1987. The test trench at el-Araj revealed only one level of occupation, and that was from the fourth to sixth centuries A.D. (Arav 1988, 187). A few Hellenistic and medieval sherds were found, but no Hellenistic or Roman city was revealed. The probe at et-Tell, on the other hand, uncovered levels from the Early Bronze Age, the Iron Age, and the late Hellenistic/early Roman and medieval periods. Arav concluded: "In light of the finds from the probe excavations, it seems more reasonable to identify ancient Bethsaida with et-Tell than with el-Araj" (1988, 188).

The problem that et-Tell lies 1.25 miles from the Sea of Galilee appears to have been solved by geological study of the region (Shroder and Inbar 1995). A combination of processes served to remove et-Tell away from the present shore of the Sea of Galilee: (1) a recession of the water level away from the site; (2) seismic activity resulting in faulting that lifted the site away from the sea; and (3) the extension of the shoreline near the site as a result of sedimentation from flash flooding of the Jordan and other nearby rivers. It is not clear which of the three processes was the primary cause of the separation; what is clear is that et-Tell was on the edge of the Sea of Galilee in New Testament times.

Excavation at et-Tell/Bethsaida

Because of the likelihood that et-Tell is the site of Bethsaida, full-scale excavation was undertaken in 1988 (Arav 1989). Two note-worthy conclusions came from the first season of excavation. First, the basic stratigraphy of the site was established: the original set-tlement was founded in the Early Bronze Age; this was followed by an Iron Age occupation and a major Hellenistic/Roman city. Sec-ond, some finds made in the first season confirmed the identification of the site as Bethsaida: in particular, fishing tools (e.g., hooks and weights) indicated that a principal trade of the village was fishing.

Since the first season in 1988 yearly excavations have contin-ued at the site without interruption (Arav 1991, 1992, and 1995). Three areas (A, B, C) were plotted for excavation. In those areas seven levels of habitation have been unearthed (Arav 1995, 6). Each level contains one or more occupational layers. The levels are numbered I–VII from top to bottom, the sequence in which they were exposed.

Level I covers the period from the beginning of the Middle Ages (c. A.D. 500) to the present. Although no settlement was discovered on the tell itself, medieval potsherds and coins were found in the course of digging. The most significant find from the period was a Mamluk drum uncovered at the foot of the mound during the 1989 season (Arav 1993).

Level II comprises four occupation layers from the Hellenistic and early Roman periods (fourth century B.C. to first century A.D.). Bethsaida was a major site in Galilee during this time, and remains from it have been found over the entire tell. The site was proba-bly destroyed by the Romans in the Jewish War of A.D. 66–73.

Level III spans the Babylonian and Persian periods (c. 586–332 B.C.). Very little has been found from this time. Of significance are a few coins from the fifth and fourth centuries, including a Tyrian silver coin (Arav 1995, 33).

Levels IV–VI consist of strata from Iron Age II (1000–586 B.C.). During this time Bethsaida was part of the land of Geshur, a small kingdom to the north of Israel. In the tenth century, King David of Israel married the daughter of Talmai, the Geshurite king (2 Sam. 3:2–3). One of the offspring of this union, which was likely a treaty marriage, was Absalom, who later sought refuge in Geshur after slaying his half-brother Amnon (2 Sam. 13:37).

Given its size and location, Bethsaida may have served as the capital of Geshur. Thus it may have been Bethsaida where Absalom fled and lived for three years. In any event, a large complex from the time—including a temple, a plaza, and a palace—has been found at the site (Arav 1992, 253).

Level VII, the earliest level at Bethsaida, is from the Early Bronze Age. There appears to have been uninterrupted occupation from Early Bronze I (c. 3200–2800 B.C.) through Early Bronze II (c. 2800–2600 B.C.). The settlement was fortified by a thick wall made of huge boulders. The height of the wall has survived in some places to 1.30 meters (=4.25 feet) (Rousseau and Arav 1995, 21).

Ceramic Evidence

The strata of Bethsaida have been dated by the pottery remains found in them. While many of the ceramic finds have not as yet been published, a general picture can be gleaned from the preliminary reports (Arav 1995). Some of the periods, however, have been dealt with little or not at all. Our presentation is therefore limited to the major levels at the site: the Iron Age and the Hellenistic/early Roman periods.

The pottery uncovered in the Iron Age layers is typical. Characteristic jugs, jars, cooking pots, kraters, bowls, and lamps have been unearthed and thus make dating of the strata secure. Most of these vessels parallel forms found in other Iron Age II settlements, such as Megiddo, Hazor, Tell Beit Mirsim, and Jemmeh (Amiran 1970, 191–293). The only difference between the Bethsaida ware and that of the other sites is that some of the vessels have a distinct texture (Arav 1995, 25). The clay is dark because it contains large amounts of basalt grits.

The ceramics from the Hellenistic/early Roman periods are commonly divided into two categories, fine ware and common ware. The earliest Hellenistic pottery discovered at the site is black Athenian ware from the mid-fourth century B.C. The latest pottery is Herodian oil lamps that date to the first century B.C. (Arav 1995, 19).

The fine ware found at Bethsaida is predominantly Hellenistic from the second century B.C. A few examples are early Roman from the first century B.C. "The Bethsaida fragments compare favorably with parallels from Hellenistic and Roman layers at different sites" (Fortner 1995, 106). There is little that is uncommon or rare.

The common ware from Bethsaida is also quite similar to that found at other sites with Hellenistic/early Roman remains. A study of the cooking pots confirms the parallels (Tessaro 1995). For example, a cooking pot with a short neck and a lid found at Bethsaida is "abundantly paralleled throughout the Galilee, where it is the most common type of cookpot in the late first century B.C. and first century A.D. assemblages" (Berlin 1988, 61–62).

Architectural Remains

As would be expected, the principal building remains come from Levels IV–VI (Iron Age II) and Level II (Hellenistic/early Roman). The most important architectural finds for the Iron Age emerged in Areas A and B, where, at the top of the tell, once stood a large building complex. In Area A a monumental structure that perhaps served as a temple was unearthed. In front of the gate of this building was a row of erect basalt stones (maṣṣĕbôt) probably used for worship. Also in front of the huge building was a large, paved plaza apparently connected with the threshold.

In Area B was found a palace from Iron Age II. It was constructed according to the Assyrian-Aramean style called bit hilani. Apparently facing the plaza to the south, the palace contained a throne room and storage rooms. The structure "is built very massively of large boulders and thick walls. Some of the boulders weigh over a ton, and the average width of the walls is 1.4 meters. The palace is not yet fully excavated; so far an area measuring 27.5 by 25 meters has been unearthed" (Arav 1995, 24).

A residence characteristic of the Hellenistic/early Roman period was also excavated in Area B. A large building (18 by 27 meters), it was erected around a central courtyard in the manner typical of the times. The owners were probably fishermen, as is evident from numerous fishing implements, such as needles and weights, discovered in the house (Rousseau and Arav 1995, 22). And thus its name—the Fisherman's House (Arav 1992, 254).

In Area A was found an oval structure constructed of massive boulders. Measuring 7 by 5.5 meters, the installation probably served as a granary during the Hellenistic/early Roman period.

A monumental gate was found on the eastern side of the tell in the 1997 season. It had a paved entranceway with *maṣṣĕbôt* standing near the entrance. Further excavation work will determine the date of the gate and its precise form.

Small Finds

Small finds vary by site. An agriculturally based settlement will yield sickles, plowshares, and the like; a fishing village will yield anchors, needles, and net weights. Tells that were occupied only in the Bronze Age do not have coins, whereas sites occupied during Roman times have a lot.

In keeping with these principles, no coins were found in the Iron Age levels at Bethsaida (IV–VI). On the other hand, many coins were discovered in the layers of the Hellenistic/early Roman period and following. "Since excavations began in 1987, some seventy-six coins have been discovered that cover a wide range of history, from a fifth-century BCE Tyrian Obol to nineteenth- and twentieth-century coins from the Ottoman empire" (Strickert 1995, 165).

The Iron Age levels have yielded a few choice finds. One is an Aramaic ostracon with the name "Aqiba" incised on it. Also, a molded clay figurine that appears to be a male wearing a crown was found in the large public structure (Arav 1995, 17).

The Hellenistic/early Roman layers have yielded many more small finds than has any other period. A clay seal picturing a boat with two men standing in it was found in Area A. From the same area came a clay figurine of a female with curled hair and a veil. From Area C numerous small finds came forth, such as iron sickles, a gold earring, and a strigil. And, of course, as already mentioned, excavation of Level II brought to light fishing gear (sewing needles, net weights, and hooks) in various areas of the site. These small finds lend weight to the thesis that et-Tell is the site of the fishing village/city of Bethsaida.

We have seen that all the methods of archaeology discussed in previous chapters are relevant to the excavation of Bethsaida. They are all necessary, and they all work together to provide material for a reconstruction of the history of the site. Bethsaida is coming back to life by means of archaeology. It is our hope that this brief study has given the reader a taste of how archaeology works and perhaps a desire to do some work in the field.

Bibliography

Amiran, R. 1970. *Ancient Pottery of the Holy Land*. New Brunswick, N.J.: Rutgers University Press.

Arav, R. 1988. "Et-Tell and el-Araj." *IEJ* 38:187–88.

———. 1989. "Et-Tell, 1988." *IEJ* 39:99–100.

———. 1991. "Bethsaida, 1989." *IEJ* 41:184–85.

———. 1992. "Bethsaida, 1992." *IEJ* 42:252–54.

———. 1993. "A Mamluk Drum from Bethsaida." *IEJ* 43:241–45.

———. 1995. "Bethsaida Excavations: Preliminary Report." In R. Arav and R. Freund, eds., *Bethsaida: A City by the North Shore of the Sea of Galilee*, 3–63. Kirksville, Mo.: Thomas Jefferson University Press.

Avi-Yonah, M. 1977. *The Holy Land: From the Persian to the Arab Conquest*. Grand Rapids: Baker.

Berlin, A. 1988. *The Hellenistic and Early Roman Common-Ware Pottery from Tel-Anfa*. Ann Arbor: University Microfilms.

Fortner, S. 1995. "Hellenistic and Roman Fineware from Bethsaida." In R. Arav and R. Freund, eds., *Bethsaida*, 99–126. Kirksville, Mo.: Thomas Jefferson University Press.

Freund, R. 1995. "The Search for Bethsaida in Rabbinic Literature." In R. Arav and R. Freund, eds., *Bethsaida*, 267–311. Kirksville, Mo.: Thomas Jefferson University Press.

Kuhn, H., and R. Arav. 1991. "Bethsaida Excavations: Historical and Archaeological Approaches." In *The Future of Early Christianity*, ed. B. Pearson et al., 77–107. Minneapolis: Fortress.

McCown, C. 1930. "The Problem of the Site of Bethsaida." *JPOS* 10:32–58.

Pixner, B. 1985. "Searching for the New Testament Site of Bethsaida." *BA* 48.4:207–16.

Rousseau, J., and R. Arav. 1995. *Jesus and His World*. Minneapolis: Fortress.

Shroder, J. F., and M. Inbar. 1995. "Geologic and Geographic Background to the Bethsaida Excavations." In R. Arav and R. Freund, eds., *Bethsaida*, 65–98. Kirksville, Mo.: Thomas Jefferson University Press.

Smith, R. W. 1993. "Jesus' Not Quite So Galilean Ministry." Paper presented at the forty-fifth annual meeting of the Evangelical Theological Society, Nov. 18–20, at Washington, D.C.

Strange, J. F. 1992. "Bethsaida." *ABD* 1:692–93.

Strickert, F. 1995. "The Coins of Philip." In R. Arav and R. Freund, eds., *Bethsaida*, 165–89. Kirksville, Mo.: Thomas Jefferson University Press.

Tessaro, T. 1995. "Hellenistic and Roman Ceramic Cooking Ware from Bethsaida." In R. Arav and R. Freund, eds., *Bethsaida*, 127–39. Kirksville, Mo.: Thomas Jefferson University Press.

Wilkinson, J. 1977. *Jerusalem Pilgrims before the Crusades*. Warminster, Eng.: Aris and Phillips.

Notes

Notes to Chapter 3: "The Tales of Tells"

1. Joe D. Seger, on his first visit to Tell Halif (which he would later excavate), explained how he knew it was an occupation mound: "The identifying configurations were the mound's sizeable flat surface on top and its regularly sloping sides. The flatness indicated successive building layers; the sloping sides, ancient fortification walls beneath the surface" (Cole 1977, 32).

2. *Tell* is an Arabic word meaning "hill." Its plural is *tulul*. The modern Hebrew equivalent is *tel*, as in Tel Aviv. Early British publications used *tall* for an occupation mound, but that spelling is now obsolete.

3. Early translators of the Bible were not aware that the Hebrew *tel* referred to an occupied mound. They believed it was a word for "strength" (Wright 1962b, 23). So the King James translates: "But as for the cities that stood still in their strength, Israel burned none of them, save Hazor only." The reader might also consider Deut. 13:16; Josh. 8:28; and Jer. 49:2.

4. William Stiebing (1981) provocatively suggests that Thomas Jefferson was the first to recognize strata in a mound.

5. Paul Lapp reported he had discovered seventeen pits in a single excavation area at Tell Taʿannek. It was also recently told to me that a salvage project at Tel Motza outside of Jerusalem had uncovered fifty storage pits in an area about 100 by 40 meters.

Notes to Chapter 4: "Living by Site (Surveying)"

1. For a general discussion of methodology in archaeological surveying see Schiffer, Sullivan, and Klinger 1978, and Ruppe 1966.

2. E.g., Glueck's later work had less depth than did his earlier surveys: "Much of his later work was carried out from a jeep, without the on-foot, meter-by-meter investigation required of archaeological field surveys today" (Levy 1995, 47).

Notes to Chapter 7: "Petrie, Pottery, and Potsherds"

1. The first publication to deal with the chronological significance of painted pottery was A. Furtwängler and G. Loeschcke, *Mykenische Thongefässe* (Berlin: Asher, 1879). The value of unpainted pottery, or what is sometimes called kitchenware, was first deduced by Petrie at Tell el-Hesi in 1890.

2. A slip can also be produced when pottery is fired: particles rise to the surface and change the color of the vessel.

3. For a study of biblical words and ideas dealing with pottery, see Kelso 1948.

Note to Chapter 10: "Archaeology in Use: The Recovery of Bethsaida"

1. Even recently some scholars have accepted this position. See Pixner 1985.

Index